My Life in Japanese Art and Gardens

The author, Adachi Zenko.

My Life in Japanese Art and Gardens

From Entrepreneur to Connoisseur

The Autobiography of Adachi Zenko,
Founder of the Adachi Museum of Art

Translated by Giles Murray

Stone Bridge Press • Berkeley, California

Published by
Stone Bridge Press
P.O. Box 8208
Berkeley, CA 94707
TEL 510-524-8732 • sbp@stonebridge.com • www.stonebridge.com

The word order of Japanese names follows current usage, family name first.

Originally published in Japanese as *Teien Nihon-ichi: Adachi Bijutsukan o Tsukutta Otoko* by Adachi Zenko. ©2007 Adachi Museum of Art. Published by arrangement with Nikkei Publishing Inc., Tokyo, Japan.

All photographs and illustrations used by permission of Adachi Museum of Art.

Illustrations on chapter part-title pages by Adachi Zenko.

Jacket and text design by Linda Ronan.

Printed in the United States of America.

2013 2012 2011 2010 2009   10 9 8 7 6 5 4 3 2 1

Library of Congress Cataloging-in-Publication Data is available from the publisher.

ISBN 978-1-933330-86-0

Contents

Introduction

I was born the eldest son in a family of small tenant farmers in Iinashi in the Nogi district of Shimane Prefecture in western Japan. Part of what is called the San'in region and known as Izumo Province many centuries ago, this area was once one of the power centers of the whole country. We lived about 5 miles from the center of Yasugi, a town famous for its *yasugibushi* folk music and for its *dojosukui* rustic dance.

I tumbled into the world on February 8, 1899, the year of the wild boar in the Chinese zodiac. Fortunetellers say that people born in this year are aggressive by nature. Reckless and foolhardy, they are prone to charge full speed ahead without thinking first. This makes sense, I suppose, because in Japanese, 猪, the character for wild boar, is often found in words associated with having a devil-may-care attitude. Looking back on my life now at the age of ninety, I see that I was a typically wild and impetuous product of the year I was born.

I wasn't the sharpest tool in the shed. No sooner had I graduated from my small village elementary school than I began to help out on my family's farm. In those days, everyone in a tenant farmer's family—women, children, old folks—divided the work up among them. If the entire family didn't pitch in, it would have been a struggle to pay the yearly rice tax, and you wouldn't have had enough to eat. But those were difficult days for tenant farmers. Their demands for land improvements and a reform to field divisions put them at loggerheads with the landowning class.

I worked like a dog from morning until night. Since I was a child fresh out of elementary school, all the farm gear—hoes, plows, and straw raincoats—was way too big for me, but still, I liked nothing better than the grown-ups telling me I was a hard worker and doing a great job despite my age. Encouragement like that inspired me to work harder.

The rice paddies weren't enough to live off, so in the off-season I would earn a little extra money by loading up a handcart with charcoal and hauling it through the bitterly cold, snow-covered roads. This was around the end of the Meiji and the start of the Taisho period, or about 1912 in the Western calendar. Since then I've done so many different jobs that all my fingers and toes together aren't enough to count them!

Cart hauler, charcoal seller, shellfish wholesaler, stall manager, rice broker, general-store owner, charcoal briquette salesman, textile wholesaler, sword maker, car salesman, kindergarten operator, real estate dealer—and that's just a rough list off the top of my head! Add them all up properly and the total would be somewhere north of thirty. Frankly, I'm astonished that I managed to work in so many trades, both in Osaka and back home, without really knowing anything.

I can still remember all the different episodes of my life, sometimes nostalgically, sometimes not. Every job I had had its own unique pleasures and pains. The fact that I can remember events from seventy or even eighty years ago shows how intense they were.

As a child I was a hopelessly thick student, a dropout quite unable to keep up with everybody else. My grades were always second—*from the bottom*, that is. It's probably hard to imagine from the in-your-face way I carry on nowadays, but back in the day I was a shy, quiet lad—such a timid little milksop, in fact, that even the girls made fun of me. I loathed and detested school, and my daily whining about not wanting to go must have caused my parents no end of grief. When the time came for me to graduate, I got my certification thanks to a lenient, good-natured teacher who felt that it would be downright cruel to fail a student as quiet and serious as I was, no matter how bad my grades.

I couldn't get over my sense of being worthless and inferior, so I moped a lot. Why was I so stupid when all my sisters were so brainy? I even began to entertain suspicions that my mother had had an affair of which I was the outcome! I eventually realized that I could agonize all I liked, but it wasn't going to make me a whit brainier. Strangely enough, this realization inspired me to try my hand at all sorts of things regardless of the obstacles. My only watchwords were "hard work" and "perseverance."

At the age of twenty, I joined the 63rd Matsue Infantry Regiment for a two-year stint. I can see, in hindsight, that this was when I picked up the know-how and self-confidence to make my way through life.

Since no one from my village had ever risen to the rank of private first class, I was determined to do so. I took the initiative, polishing the boots and washing the underwear of all the squad leaders, fetching water, and generally sucking up to my superior officers. In old Japanese warrior terms I was like the ambitious underling Toyotomi Hideyoshi currying favor with the warlord Oda Nobunaga. And I managed to achieve my goal. I was made private first class and returned to my village very proud of myself indeed. This experience taught me something that became one of my cast-iron beliefs: "If you really believe in what you're doing, then you can achieve it, whatever it is."

I wasn't clever and I didn't have any money. I had nothing to lose, which, I suppose, was an advantage. Perhaps having nothing and having nothing to fear are one and the same. As soon as I had made up my mind, I acted. Some people don't do what they say they're going to, but I always did exactly what I said I would. I still have the same single-mindedness and optimism today. Be prepared to bet your life on what you believe in—that's my stance 100 percent of the time.

Luckily for me, I always liked working and was blessed with good health. And once I had learned the lesson that the harder you exert yourself, the more you earn, I worked with complete focus. A fool judges everything by the one thing he knows. For me that yardstick was money, money, and . . . money. Making money meant everything to me. What I most enjoyed was lying in bed and drifting off to sleep while cooking up my next moneymaking scheme. At the same time, it slowly dawned on me that the secret of business success was giving top priority to relationships.

The first and most important thing is to be trusted. Next, you must never, ever let anyone down. If you make money for someone once, afterward they'll always be happy to lend you what you need.

One of my patented skills is the mastery of getting a loan, know-how that's the result of my having no capital in the first place. "Credit is infinite wealth" goes the old saying, and it's true.

Knowing that I was none too bright made me feisty and defiant and played a big part in making me the man I am. No matter what sort of trouble I got into, it usually took me less than a year to wriggle out of it. Other people were amazed by my strength in adversity and the way I got back up no matter how many times I was knocked down. I think they'd all be more amazed if they knew that the secret source of my unstoppable energy was my knowledge that I was not too smart—strange but true. I like the line about how your greatest strength is what you *don't* have. I always carry my school report card around with me in my jacket pocket to make sure I never forget my old innocent self.

"Art, women, and Japanese gardens—that's the story of my life" is how I like to sum myself up. All three things are beautiful, and they're a perfect match for my life philosophy, which has always been to follow my dreams. There are plenty of things I am hopeless at, but when it comes to these three I can hold my own with anybody.

In Buddhism, it's traditional to get a new name, called *kai-myo*, after your death, and I gave myself the death name 美術院高色庭園居士, or *bijutsuin-koshoku-teien-koji*. This name says that I'm an art collector, an incorrigible lady's man, and an expert garden designer. Inscribe this on a tombstone and everyone will know right away that it's mine.

I may have already chosen my own death name, but I never give a moment's thought to death itself. There are so many things I still want to do. That is why I am praying busily to the Lord of the Dead and asking him to stay his hand for a couple of years or so. Once those years are up, I'll just request another postponement. He is someone with whom I try to remain on friendly, but distant, terms!

In spring last year, Death and I had an encounter that was a little too close for comfort when I found myself having to have an operation at the ripe age of ninety. It was a dangerous procedure. The doctor himself told me that no one my age had ever had this operation. My family and friends all made a great song and dance, but I was quite relaxed about it. I had been praying to the Lord of the Dead, and had taken good care to give him his mid- and end-year offerings so he'd take care of me in return. Deep inside my mind, I could hear him whispering, "Go on! Live a long time." More than that though, I hadn't any intention of fading quietly away.

"Always have a dream to follow or you'll end up a moron." This is something I always say to other people, but it's good advice for me too. In life, passion and desire to do things make us who we are and give us energy. It's only when a person starts to be satisfied with the status quo that he starts to get old.

✦ ✦ ✦

In April last year, the new Ceramics Hall was finished, adding a whole new dimension to the Adachi Museum of Art. On display are pieces by Kawai Kanjiro and Kitaoji Rosanjin, the greatest potters in contemporary Japan. In a corner of the Kawai Room, we have built an *irori* sunken hearth to evoke a traditional arts-and-crafts atmosphere, while the Rosanjin Room is in the style of an elegant restaurant or *ryotei* with a round tea room–style window to express his belief that fine dining is an integrated art of food, ceramic dishes, and interior design. I also hope that museum visitors will look through the Ceramics Hall window to enjoy the panorama of the garden. I believe that an exhibition space should always complement the exhibits.

What I'm most excited about right now is my plan to construct a contemporary art museum to capture the spirit of art today. I've already built the world's finest replica Japanese castle, a 70-foot structure on Mount Kanao. And I haven't abandoned my dream of reconstructing the fabled Toda Castle in nearby Hirose, a quaint Kamakura-like town near where I was raised and to which I am deeply attached.

I'm also very keen to invite some important figures from overseas to my museum. I want to contribute to international friendship and understanding by spreading an awareness of Japan's splendid culture. Even if I don't manage to achieve this in my own lifetime, I hope that my children and grandchildren will.

Another project I'm looking into is the construction of the world's finest conference center and hotel on Mount Noroyama in Higashi Izumocho, about ten minutes from the Adachi Museum by car. This is the best way to help the world perceive Japan as a nation with a sophisticated culture.

A little haiku I composed not long ago expresses my current state of mind:

> Though I have climbed
> The ninety-year hill,
> My dreams go on

I've always been greedy, and I've failed miserably countless times because I let greed run away with me. On the other hand, my good nature has sometimes worked against me—I've been the victim of quite a few swindlers. I've sold whole companies for the price of a bag of garbage; had them swiped from right under my nose; bled seas of red ink investing in art; and more. Since I sowed the seeds it was only fair for me to reap the whirlwind, but mine has still been a life of painful struggle and setbacks.

Yamanaka Shikanosuke, one of the ten bodyguards of Amago Yoshihisa, a Japanese warlord from the late 16th and early 17th centuries, famously said, "Grant me seven trials, then eight tribulations." I'm not as much of a masochist as he was, but still I had to plow my way through ordeal after ordeal.

How has a person like me managed to make it so far? I was lucky enough to meet some marvelous people. That may sound obvious, but I've only figured it out now at my great age. That's how obtuse I am.

I'm the sort of person who can start a business, but can't build it up. I'm not much good at following through. And that's when the people around me step in and help out. I'm very aware that I owe all my success to them. I truly believe that "people are your best asset."

The writer Yoshikawa Eiji liked to say, "Everyone in this

world is my mentor and my teacher." I agree 100 percent. After all, we're all part of society. No one can live his life without other people.

Life isn't a smooth ride for anyone. There comes a time when the going gets rough and obstacles—whether sheer cliffs or bottomless ravines—block your path. When you're at your wits' end, you find out who you really are. You change, taking on the qualities of different creatures of the Chinese zodiac.

I may be proud to think of myself as a wild boar, but I can also work as hard as a mouse, be as crafty and clever as a monkey, or plod determinedly forward like a horse pulling a cart. One minute, I can be as stolid as an ox or as mild as a rabbit or a sheep, only to turn on people as fiercely as a dragon or a tiger. It's these sorts of shifts that make us human. And the twelve creatures of the zodiac offer us such a range of choices.

"Time shoots by like an arrow" and "The months and days are the travelers of eternity" are sayings expressing the notion that life just flies by. To be perfectly honest, I don't think I've learned anything profound or gained any special insights simply because of my age, but ninety years is a very, very long time. To borrow a line from the great haiku poet Matsuo Basho, my dreams are most certainly "running around on the parched plains," but mine are not the fleeting, delicate dreams of the poet. I've groped my way through darkness and done well to get where I am today. Though I say it myself, I think I deserve a round of applause.

At the urging of my family and friends, I decided to tell the story of my life. I started trying to write an autobiography several years ago, jotting down notes in a school notebook in my little room above the Osaka office, but I gave up in despair about halfway through—the thought of working my way through a life as long as mine made me feel faint—and couldn't get back into the swing of it. "Just write the book as if you were telling us your favorite stories about the old days, the way you always do," my grandchildren said. "There's still so much we don't know about you. Why not take the opportunity to pull it all together." That didn't sound too difficult, so I felt my interest coming back. I'm not confident writing about politics, education, or economics, but I am when it comes to art, gardens, or bawdy tales.

I am a sucker for flattery; it's a bad habit. If people tell me that the museum garden is fantastic, I want to please them more by making it even better. Same thing when I get complimented on the size and quality of my Yokoyama Taikan collection— I get fired up to acquire even more of his works. I'm quick to become excited and enthusiastic about things. It's what made me ambitious, and it may well be the secret of a long life, too.

My life, as I said earlier, can be summed up in three words—paintings, women, and gardens. Of course, there was a lot of other stuff, too, but I don't think you'd enjoy it if I yammered on endlessly about all the hard times I've been through. Equally, if I simply bragged about what a fine fellow I am, while it might cheer me up, it wouldn't be much fun to read.

Recently, people I have met have asked me, "Why did you open a museum?" Are you in it for the money? Do you want to give something back to society? Or is it just a hobby? It seems to be a matter of burning curiosity for them. I always say that I'm in it for *all three* reasons. I really am a greedy fellow! But ultimately, I suppose, I'm doing it because I like it.

I want to take you on a haphazard journey through my life with its successes and failures, as well my obsessions with paintings, women, and gardens. Here it all is: my childhood, the work I've done, the people I've met.

Forgive me if my feelings sometimes get the better of me and I start to brag and boast in an irritating way. Feel free to dismiss such passages as the jabbering of a silly, old man.

Illustrations on chapter part-title pages by Adachi Zenko.

The Budding
of a Male Oshin

My birth name was Adachi Yoshimoto, like Imagawa Yoshimoto, the famous warlord from the Warring States period of the 1500s. And that's the name in all my school reports. I am sorry to say I never got around to asking my parents why they chose to call me that, but at the age of twenty-four I officially changed my name from Yoshimoto to Zenko, the name I still use. I did it on the advice of an onomast, a kind of fortune-teller specializing in names, after the collapse of a business I'd set up in Yonago.

I'm not particularly superstitious, but I liked Zenko. It sounds nice and has positive associations. The *ko* bit sounds like the old Japanese word for "top marks" or "A grade," and the word *zenko,* when written with different characters, can also mean "good deeds."

In 1970, when I was seventy-one, I constructed the Adachi Museum of Art in Yasugi, my birthplace in Shimane Prefecture. This act fulfilled a desire I'd long had to give something back to my hometown. I saw it as a "good deed" that had its origins in my new name.

There is no denying the fact that I feel attached to my birth name. After all, it's easy to change your name, but impossible to change who you are. My memories of the time when I was Yoshimoto are as vivid as ever. In fact, I suspect that it could be my having changed my name, rather than the passage of time, that makes me look back on my youth so fondly. After all, who ever forgets the first flowering of their emotions?

So when did my feelings put out their first buds? More than eighty years have gone by, but I'm pretty sure it was when I was a fourth grader and fell in love with a girl who had recently transferred to my school. This first experience of love transformed my view of the world. It gave me an almighty shock— like a bird that's been hit by a peashooter.

Until that moment my grades had been terrible, I had been horribly shy, and I hated going to school more than anything. Indifferent to everything, I drifted aimlessly through life. Then, one day I fell in love with this girl. It was a seismic event. Not only did I now enjoy going to school, but my whole life was galvanized. It felt great. The instant I woke up, I wanted nothing more than to speed off to school as fast as I could. Looking back on it now, I'm a little shocked at the speed of my transformation. The experience taught me something about myself: Though I was hopeless at schoolwork, when it came to women I had the same feelings as everyone else.

Her name was Ishii Kunie. Petite and clever, she was a real class act. I was madly in love and used to dream about her night after night. Though I was crazy about her, I didn't have the guts to tell her. A classic case of hopeless one-sided love, it was fun all the same. A glimpse of her face was enough to make me happy. She had a beautiful smile, and I used to practice grinning in the mirror in an effort to keep up with her.

"Kunie. Kunie." I remember repeating her name over and over. She once called out to me in the school corridor. I stopped, blushed furiously, and the world went blank before my eyes. I was as pale and feverish as if I had measles. Any one of these symptoms shows that at least in matters of the heart I was sure to get a passing grade.

After spending her whole life in Yasugi, Kunie died not long ago in her eighties. When I was profiled on a TV program called *Nihon no Shacho* ("Japan's Corporate Leaders") in 1980, I persuaded her to join me on the show. That was when I finally got around to telling her I'd once been in love with her. It only took me a little more than seventy years to reveal my true feelings!

When we got in touch to tell her we were on our way over to her house with the TV crew, she begged for more time so she could change into a formal kimono. She sounded quite panicky.

"No, no, no," I told her. "It'll be much better if you just

wear your normal, everyday clothes. Don't make a big deal of it. Just make sure to be at home when we come around. It'll be fine." I managed to persuade her, and she was filmed wearing a Japanese-style apron. Still, the experience made me see how women always want to look their best, no matter what age they are.

The presenter of the show was Miyao Susumu, a TV personality. He cracked lots of jokes and kept us all in stitches. Getting in the spirit of the thing, I took hold of Kunie's right hand and kissed it. Despite being in her eighties, she reacted with such girlish embarrassment that everyone burst out laughing. The following day she sent me a Kewpie doll in a lovely costume she had sewn herself. It was a marvelous first romance in its own peculiar way and about the only ray of sunshine in a childhood that was more about endurance than enjoyment.

✧ ✧ ✧

My childhood had a lot in common with *Oshin*, the TV series that was such a big hit some years ago. In fact, the story of the indomitable and persevering title character, growing up in the early 20th century and enduring all kinds of mistreatment, is so similar to my own that I feel it could have been modeled on my life. I am a big fan of Hashida Sugako, the author of the book on which the show was based. "How did you research the life and customs of the time?" I asked her when she came to visit my museum. "I mean, it's all so well done. I get the feeling you were there yourself and lived Oshin's life with her."

"I belong to the last generation whose mothers were born in the Meiji period," Hashida explained. "And I always believed that telling the life story of Oshin, a sort of nameless everywoman, could provide us with pointers for living our own lives. I had my mother's and my mother-in-law's letters, and people sent me others that women all over Japan had written in the Meiji, Taisho, and Showa periods. Oshin is a composite of all their experiences." It struck me that a drama as touching as *Oshin* is always written from the heart, not the head. That explains why it has affected so many people so powerfully.

I watched it faithfully every day, projecting my own childish self onto the main character. I got more caught up in it than any other recent program I can think of. Of course, Oshin was a clever, modest, and pretty girl, while I, her male counterpart, was rather stupid and most certainly not pretty. I had nothing going for me at all, making my life that much more difficult.

✦ ✦ ✦

I'm doing my best to describe my childhood, but I barely have any memories of my life before elementary school. My earliest memory is the distant booming of cannon fire during the Russo-Japanese War. It was May 27, 1905, the first day of the Battle of Tsushima, and the sound of the Japanese engaging the Russian Baltic fleet reached my school. I remember being terribly afraid. Years later I found out that some of the crew of a camouflaged Russian cruiser that sank in the battle were washed up not too far away in Naga and Mino in Shimane Prefecture.

I was born on February 8, 1899, at 320 Oaza Furukawa in the village of Iinashi, Nogi district, in Shimane Prefecture. The house where I was born stood near the stone lantern in the middle of the Pond Garden of the present Adachi Museum of Art. Directly opposite our house was Saginoyu Onsen, a hot spring where in ancient times a heron (*sagi* means "heron" in Japanese) was supposed to have fluttered down to treat its wounds.

Iinashi was a typical agricultural village on the southwest of the Nogi plain and around 13 miles from Matsue. The Iinashi River flowed via Hirose and Yasugi into Lake Nakaumi. When

I was born, the village had a little more than 440 households and a population slightly more than 2,000. Furukawa, where we lived, was a minuscule sub-hamlet with only 25 homes.

According to our region's ancient chronicle, *Izumo Fudoki*, the name Iinashi derives from the deity Okunitama no Mikoto having eaten in this region—*ii* means "meal," and *nashi* "eat"—although the characters used in the name were changed in A.D. 726 and no longer reflect this. But there's no need to consult the old texts to see that it's been a farming region since time immemorial. The sheer number of people with surnames that include the element *ta* or *da*, meaning "rice paddy," is proof enough. There are Tsukadas, Haradas, Otas, Edas, Ikedas, Hirotas, Iwatas, Yoritas, Sodas, Fukadas, Hamadas, and Tabes. The area of cultivated land was small compared to the number of households, so the majority of people rented, rather than owned, their land. There were many poor peasant-farmers, which is what my family had been for generations.

My father was called Kakuichi and my mother, Tome. I was born the second of four children, all girls except me (Kame, Kumano, and Yasuko, in descending order). That made me the eldest son and heir of the Adachi family. Since my grandfather Seizo and grandmother Mon were still alive and well, there were eight of us in the family all told. Although it is a large family by today's standards, it was normal for the end of the Meiji period.

Our house was a very rough-and-ready affair with a thatched roof and walls coated with clay. The focal point was an earth-floored kitchen with an area equivalent to about 15 tatami mats;* there were three more rooms of 8, 8, and 4.5 mats, respectively, while the bathroom and the toilet were outside. A stream ran through our garden, and we used it to wash our agricultural tools and the vegetables we ate. There were always chickens hopping about; I vaguely remember them picking at their food on the ground. In those days most people

---

* About 270 square feet. 1 tatami is 0.5 *tsubo* = 17.8 square feet; an actual tatami is roughly twice as long as it is wide.

had a clump of bamboo around their houses as a fence; we had a row of bamboo behind ours to conceal it.

On our very modest patch of land, a piece of mountainside and some fields, we grew rice and barley, as well as sweet potatoes, *daikon* radishes, eggplant, taro, Chinese cabbage, and soybeans, depending on the season. But since our harvest was just enough for the family to subsist on, we had to rent more fields from a big landowner in order to make a proper living.

Our main food was a combination of rice and barley in a 6:4 ratio. At times, both our daily meals consisted of dumplings and *yakimeshi* (powdered rice, corn, and buckwheat noodles). On occasion, we would mix in a large amount of tofu lees (residue from the production of tofu or soymilk) with the rice to trick ourselves into thinking we had eaten well. We usually had salted fish, boiled vegetables, or pickles. I had to be ill before anyone would even think about letting me have a luxury like an egg! We would all sit on a straw mat spread on the earthen floor and eat our meal beside the fire beneath the feeble glow of a single lamp. Since coarse food and clothing were the norm, we were all surprisingly cheerful.

The Adachi is the head family in their family clan, but as far as I can tell no one from the either the main or cadet branches of the family had ever made any money. None of the graves are anything special, and some of the tombstones are little more than a heap of rocks. The death register mentions my ancestors only as far back as Seizo's father, Mosuke, who died at the age of seventy-four on March 15, 1896. All documentation of previous ancestors was destroyed when Shumatsu-ji, the family temple, burned down in the great Hirose fire of April 27, 1915.

Although I don't remember much about my childhood, that doesn't mean I was not blessed with a loving family. My father and I didn't get along, but my grandmother, grandfather, and mother could not have been kinder or more protective.

The oldest photographi I own. That is me at the right.

My grandfather Seizo belonged to the Iwata family but had taken our name when he married into our family. Since he and Mon could not have children, they had adopted Tome, Mon's sister's child. Since my father was also an adopted son-in-law from the Uchida family, I was the first male child to be born into the Adachi family in fifty years and, therefore, the source of much rejoicing. Mon, in particular, supposedly spent days on end gazing at me, smiling, as she said to herself: "You can tell from his face that he's going to be somebody special."

Seizo adored me and was as sweet to me as if I were his real grandson, though there was no blood connection between us. I'm told he used to bounce me up and down on his knee as he sipped his drink every evening. A very religious man, he loved reading books and drinking sake and was good at making things from straw. Widely liked and trusted, he was often asked to manage forest and agricultural land on behalf of landowners. If someone asked him to do something, he was unable to turn them down—something that caused him his share of problems, especially when he'd put himself up as a guarantor for other people. He had the resources to gradually buy up forest and farmland for himself. He and my grandmother got along very well, and other people became jealous when they saw my grandmother singing along as he played the shamisen, a three-stringed instrument. Even now, I still respect my grandfather Seizo more than any other person in the world.

My parents did not get along nearly as well. To put it charitably, my father was impatient and had the perfectionism typical of craftsmen. To put it less charitably, he was overbearing, dogmatic, and quick to scold me. He was always thinking about farm work, and from a child's perspective, he wasn't simply difficult and prickly, but downright frightening.

My mother, meanwhile, was a beautiful, well-proportioned woman. She was physically strong and did her work with efficiency and skill. Whenever anything happened to upset me, I would run to her arms or those of my grandfather and grandmother. As a young child, I was emotionally frail, and that didn't change much even after I went off to elementary school.

✤ ✤ ✤

I went to Iinashi Elementary School in April 1905. It was a half hour's walk from home in straw sandals along the paths through the paddy fields. The school building was a two-story wooden structure, and there must have been about two hundred students. I see from the records of the time that there were forty-two children in my year (twenty-four boys and eighteen girls), most from farming families. The classes were split according to the lower and higher years, and there were four ability levels.

My best friend at school was Adachi Inosuke. We fought, but we would always make up afterward and were as close as brothers. He spent his whole life near Iinashi. He was a very good student and three years my senior. He was always being elected class officer or sub-officer, and when the students lined up on the playground, it was his job to shout out directions. I always thought it an awesome sight.

I suppose my respect for my friend was partly about me, a bad student, wanting to be something that I wasn't. My three sisters all had good grades, and a couple of them were even appointed class leader. I was the only member of my family who performed poorly for the entire six years of school. Just once, in my third year, I got an A in ethics. But I usually got Cs in Japanese language, math, Japanese history, Japanese geography, and cooking and Bs in ethics, physical education, drawing, and singing. Since I was quiet and polite, I did better in the more content-light, behavior-based subjects. Still, I think my teachers marked up my grades in PE and singing. I was tone-deaf and always came last in races. I certainly wasn't A or B material.

Drawing was the only subject I liked. My teacher used to praise me and would occasionally hang my pictures on the classroom walls. Now and again, one of the school bullies would ask me to draw him a picture—being taken seriously like that always cheered me up no end. In fact, I have only one painful memory associated with art.

I was desperate to buy myself a book of drawing samples, but convinced that my father would only become angry if I mentioned it to him, I stole 15 *sen* from my grandfather's wallet. My grandfather was good at working with straw and would earn money to buy sake by making things like sandals. A clever man, he was also good at doing sums in his head. It didn't take him long to realize that some of his money had gone missing.

"Anybody know anything about this?" he asked the family.

I wanted to come clean, but I wasn't brave enough and in the end said nothing. Glancing up, I caught sight of my grandfather's face. During the split second that our eyes met, I realized that he knew perfectly well what had happened and was only pretending not to. I felt pangs of guilt every time I looked at the book, and I swore that I would never again help myself to anything of my family's without asking them first. Though I was a child, I learned that guilt and remorse turn pleasure attained by wrongdoing into something unbearable.

I was bitterly ashamed of myself, but this episode demonstrates how much I loved art. It's thanks to my early experiences of drawing at elementary school that art is, alongside women and gardens, one of my all-time favorite things. A passion for paintings was already there, planted deep inside me, decades before I started collecting the works of Yokoyama Taikan or began building a museum.

Except for the days when we had art class, I couldn't find it in me to enjoy school, until I fell in love in fourth grade. I was so shy and quiet that the girls, as well as the naughty boys, teased me. No one wanted me to join in their games, and when the other children were playing at sword fighting, I was always chosen to be the inept swordsman or the villain who got killed. Ditto when we played at soldiers—I was always on the side that ended up being wiped out!

Once, the school tough guy threatened to cut me with a knife. Without knowing what I was doing, I picked up stones from the road and flung them at him until he backed off, covered in bumps and bruises. I managed to keep a lid on things on that one occasion, but if I started listing all the times I was bullied as a child I could go on for days. I remember, as clearly as if it happened yesterday, freezing winter days when everyone was clustered around the warm stove, and I shivered, off by myself, in the corner of the classroom.

Unsurprisingly, mornings were awful. I fought with my parents on a daily basis about going to school. The more my parents tried to humor me, the crosser I would become—and the less I wanted to go.

Then one day I skipped school and went off to play on Mount Kikaku. (Kikaku is the mountain with the waterfall that now forms one of the views from the Adachi Museum's garden.) I must have been in second or third grade. I have no recollection of what I did up there all day, but when I saw all the other children on their way back from school, I made my way down and went back home, trying to look innocent. But I felt restless and nervous, convinced that everyone who looked at me could see what I had done. For several days I was overcome with remorse and fretted about being found out. I regretted what I had done so much that I realized I'd have been better off going to school. The experience was a good lesson, and even if I sobbed and screamed about going to school, I never played truant again.

Another unforgettable memory of my elementary school days involves a visit, for a reason I've forgotten, to a temple when I was in sixth grade. A couple hours' walk from my house, Unju-ji, an ancient Rinzai temple, stands by the Chiyofu Bridge on the Hakuta River. To this day, the temple looks the way it did in the period of the Northern and Southern Courts (1337–92). It is the twenty-seventh pilgrimage site on the Chugoku Kannon pilgrimage route, and is sometimes referred to as Tsutsuji-dera, or the Azalea Temple.

An avenue of pines some 1,000 feet long leads up to it. Along this avenue stands a porticoed gateway with huge columns, which is designated an important cultural property. Displayed on the gate is an imperial scroll written by Emperor Godaigo himself. Thanks to the temple guidebook, I can evoke the place quite vividly, yet what lodged in my memory wasn't the splendor of the temple but the dry landscape garden on the mountainside behind it. The trees were beautifully trimmed and shaped, and the contrast between the bright green and the pale gravel was intense. As I gazed at the serene scene I couldn't stop myself from sighing, "What a fabulous garden."

Until that moment I had never been touched by the sight of a garden, but this one made a powerful impression. I felt as though I'd been struck by a thunderbolt. My father was a big gardening enthusiast and would often buy plants from the garden merchant or head off to the mountains to find pines and maples that he could then plant in our little garden. People said that when it came to gardening "you can trust Kakuichi 100 percent." Perhaps the sight of the garden had moved me so because I was my father's son.

. After that I started moving the rocks in our garden around and became interested in planting. Clearly, this encounter is what first triggered my interest in gardens. By the time I was seventeen or eighteen, I would often help my father with projects like planting trees or altering the direction of the little stream that passed through our garden.

❖ ❖ ❖

When you get down to it, the experiences I had at elementary school were the foundation for the central themes of my life: art, women, and gardens. I didn't need anybody to teach me about these things. I was drawn to them spontaneously. I'm not one for deep analysis, but I do believe that the impressions you receive in unguarded moments—when your heart is naked and exposed—stay with you throughout your life.

Are you familiar with the concept of "soft learning"? Lately, everyone in Japan seems to be talking about how kids with good resumes have a great advantage in life, but I think that the worship of impractical, nerdish study has gotten out of hand. We need to redirect our attention to education of the heart and mind. Let me put myself forward as a good example—I was a loser, but that was no reason to write me off completely. A person's worth should never be decided by their grades at school.

Starting Out
as a Hauler

I am presently the director of five companies or corporate bodies. I am honorary chairman of the Adachi Museum of Art; president and chairman of Maruzen; president and chairman of Nichibi; and a nonexecutive director at Toho Industries and Shin-Osaka Tochi, a real estate company. Since leaving elementary school I've tried my hand at maybe thirty different businesses all told. A quick, back-of-an-envelope calculation shows that about 20 percent of my ventures were successful. I have no idea if that is a good track record or not.

As a starry-eyed young man I dreamed of becoming a businessman on a heroic scale. (I have the niggling sense that I have not quite achieved that ambition.) Certainly, I can never forget the first business I got involved in as it marked the starting point of my entire entrepreneurial career.

After graduating from Iinashi Elementary School in March 1911, I helped my family in the fields, since farming was how we made a living. When I first went to school, compulsory education had only extended to the fourth grade, but the law was changed in March 1907, while I was still at school, to continue it to sixth grade. While I was sorry that graduating would take me away from Kunie, my first love, I was also relieved that I'd finally be able to get away from the studies I hated so much.

The problem was that with the pathetic grades I'd earned in sixth grade there was no way I could graduate. My results were hopeless. I was second from the bottom. The only reason I managed to squeeze through was because of my attitude—I had at least taken all my lessons seriously, which put the teachers on my side. Plus there was another student in the class who was so bad that they simply *had* to fail him. They felt, however, that failing both of us would reflect badly on the school.

"There is someone in this class who deserves to be failed, but we have decided to be charitable and give him a helping hand. We hope he'll do his very best in the future and not let us down." The teacher looked right at me as he said this in front of the whole class. I blushed furiously. I'd gotten through—but only by the skin of my teeth.

And thus it was that I ended up going out to work in the fields with my mother and father. I was twelve years old, but at a little more than 4-foot-3 still very much a child. Boys in those days wore a baggy-sleeved jacket, cotton trousers or long johns held up by a sash, and gaiters. Girls dressed similarly, but with a different kind of sash, an apron, and gauntlets that covered the backs of their hands and their wrists. A straw raincoat, a spade, and a hoe were the tools of my trade. Unable to use them properly yet, I had to bend double to do my work, a posture that brought tears of pain to my eyes. But I was lucky enough to be healthy, so I toiled away without moaning. I also preferred it to studying by a long shot. I detested schoolwork from the bottom of my heart.

My father was an extremely serious man whose hobbies were collecting loose change in a wooden box and taking care of his garden. He had enormous respect for hard work, and the amount of care he put into any job he did bordered on ridiculous. Whether transplanting rice or planting seeds, weeding, or harvesting, he went about it all as though he were creating a work of art.

His approach was very methodical on the surface, but a total disaster from the point of view of efficiency. Every task took an age to complete, and we often ended up the only family still out in the fields while all our neighbors were already enjoying their dinner. In our village, we were always the last to bring in the harvest. When things were really bad, we had to work literally until midnight, with my three sisters rubbing their sleepy eyes and whimpering. His daughters' suffering was enough to make even my father feel a little guilty, and he would try to cheer us up by saying, "Not much longer now. When we've got the harvest in, I'll give you some nice potato tempura. And a nice bit of fish to go with it, too." He didn't mean it. He never kept his promises.

By comparison, my way of doing things was rough-and-ready. As far as I was concerned, efficiency was the most important thing in farm work. But though I worked twice as hard as my father, he still wasn't happy. "You're just too sloppy. It's not good enough," he would say, before ordering me to redo something for the umpteenth time. Inevitably, we quarreled constantly. My mother would step in as peacemaker and help us patch things up. My father could work very patiently, but he was quick to lose his temper. He once chased me around the house waving a club when I was well past forty!

Our family had to pay our landlord four bales of rice from a harvest of five-and-a-half bales for the annual rice tax. Working efficiently and increasing our harvest had a direct impact on our quality of life. I was keen to make our lives easier, but things were not that simple. No matter how hard we worked, having one-and-a-half bales left over for ourselves was about the best we could hope for; years when we had a single bale or less were not unusual. Farming was thankless work in which you sweated your guts out for no return. My father tried to boost our income by adding another 6 acres of land and hiring laborers, but after subtracting wages and increased working time, we were always in the red.

We lived close to the Iinashi River in an area full of sluices designed to capture the iron sands that washed down the river. As a result, the groundwater that bubbled up through the heaps of sand and mud had a terribly high concentration of iron, which was not helpful for growing rice. To make matters worse, the river was always wrecking our crops by flooding or running dry, something that made the farmers' lives hellish. Worst of all, though, were the crushing burdens of the land rent and the yearly rice tax, both of which helped trigger the subsequent tenant farmers' reform movement.

Seeing how hard my parents worked, I gradually lost all faith in farming. You slogged your guts out from dawn till dusk for zero payback. Farming was an unappealing double bill of poverty and overwork. As time went on, I couldn't stand it anymore.

I started doing day labor on the side. In those days, ironically, hard physical jobs like hauling a cart or building up embankments to prevent floods paid the best cash wages. The peasants all used to join in hefting rope baskets full of earth. Flooding was a real problem in the area. Almost every year, the Iinashi River would burst its banks and inundate the fields. There were such big floods in 1635 and 1666 that Hirose ended up underwater. More recently, in 1886, 1890, and 1918, the Ueda embankment broke, sweeping away many houses and submerging the local area.

I remember that all the men of the village were roped in to help after the Furukawa embankment, which was about 1,000 feet from our house, broke. I helped too, but was considered, at age fourteen, too young to be given a proper quota of work. I ended up competing with a younger lad to see which of us could carry the heavier load. Although I was physically small, I was confident in my own strength and thought I'd win. Contrary to my expectations, I was the first to collapse with exhaustion—and was heartily mocked by the grown-ups for my pains.

Since I couldn't work up any enthusiasm for farming and I wasn't that good at manual labor, I felt that my only option was to become a businessman. I was desperate to get as far away from farming as I possibly could. As I experienced frustration and dissatisfaction in farming, my interest in business deepened rapidly.

Around this time we were in the farming off-season, which stretched from December to February. There was work to be had hauling carts of charcoal along the Iinashi River from

Hirose, up in the mountains of Chugoku, down to the ports of Arashima and Yasugi on Lake Nakaumi. That was the business I had my eye on.

The charcoal wholesalers, in the currency of the day, would pay 2 *sen* 5 *ri* for every sack of charcoal you carried down to the retailers near Lake Nakaumi. With a lunch box full of *umeboshi* (pickled *ume*, similar to a plum) dangling from my belt, I jammed twelve sacks weighing 60 *kan* (about 495 pounds) onto my cart and dragged it along the narrow road. The nearly 7-mile journey took me five or six hours. I set out in the morning and got back home in the evening, sometimes late at night. I was still doing hard physical labor—that hadn't changed—but I loved the way I was paid in cash every day. My daily wages were 30 *sen*.

Come lunchtime, I would sit down on a clump of grass or perch on top of a little roadside shrine to the god Jizo to eat my *umeboshi*. The roadside tea shops would sell you a couple of sardines for 3 *sen*, but I never went in as I couldn't bear the idea of parting with so much money. It was cold at that time of year. Sitting for too long meant my lower back would get very cold. I'd quickly polish off my lunch and pull the cart all the faster until I started to get shooting pains in my sides. This cycle of pain caused me a great deal of grief. I also had chilblains on my hands and feet and suffered from frostbite, too.

I walked high and low searching for steady customers, but winning new business was an arduous task—the whole world seemed to be against me. As I trudged home through the pitch-black, unlighted roads, painful blood blisters forming on my feet in my worn-out straw sandals, the sight of the lights in the windows of homes would make me wonder bitterly what I had done to deserve such a miserable life. As the cart clattered along the road behind me, tears would spring to my eyes.

Circumstances were different for my closest friend, the ambitious Adachi Inosuke. Since his family was relatively well off, he had a horse-drawn carriage with which he could transport sixty sacks in one go. Hardly surprising, a gulf quickly opened up between us in terms of both profits and our level of physical exhaustion.

This disparity exasperated me no end. Then I came up with a plan—I would go into charcoal retailing myself. I bought a cargo of charcoal and sold it to people on my route as I hauled my cart from Hirose down to Yasugi. This was my first stab at business, and when it went well I earned twice what I could get for hauling the same cargo. Business was becoming an ever more appealing option.

My sisters and me, around the time I was working as a merchant trader.

By the time I was fifteen or sixteen, my parents took care of all the farm work, while I devoted myself to my businesses of hauling and selling charcoal. The only days I took off were New Year's and the Bon festival of the dead; Sundays and public holidays were ordinary workdays for me. As I became serious about my approach to business, I slowly began to win people's trust.

✣ ✣ ✣

One day I made the acquaintance of the head of the Yamaguchiya organization. He was a highflier in the local fishing world with a monopoly on the bloody clams found in Lake

Nakaumi. "You're a youngster, but you're a good lad and I admire your spirit," he told me. "It's a waste for you to go back home with nothing in your cart. How about taking some of my clams? There's a shop I sell to in Hirose, but it's a hassle for me to make deliveries every time they order. What if I let you have them at a wholesale price, so you can do business with them on your own account? I'll make sure to tell them that, from now on, they have to go through you for everything."

His proposal was a shock to me. There I was thinking that I was so high-and-mighty, and it had never crossed my mind that returning without cargo was a waste. I was young and thoughtless. His suggestion helped me realize that other people could have a good eye for opportunity. So I started selling clams in the villages en route and in Hirose, my final destination. If they were kept in the dark, the clams would stay fresh for almost a month. As the volumes I handled grew, I asked Inosuke to help out with the hauling and together we made some pretty hefty profits.

My success with clams inspired me to start selling *daikon* radishes and potatoes, too. I realized that if you put your mind to it, there were all sorts of ways to make money. I had zero talent for schoolwork, but not a bad nose for a deal—a classic case of being good at what you enjoy.

My greatest pleasure at the time was gently drifting off to sleep every night while dreaming about new ways to make money. Especially encouraging for me was the praise I got from other people, such as "You're a hard worker" and "You're a young fellow, but I've got a lot of respect for you." It was thrilling to feel that I'd been magically transformed from a dropout to an honors student.

Whenever any of the local villages had a festival, I set up a table in a corner of the shrine grounds and would hawk bananas, rather like Tora-san, the vagabond salesman from the long-running film series. In the autumn, I would gingerly make my way across the long wooden bridge over the Iinashi—it was no wider than a gymnastics balance beam—and steal off to some secret spots I knew to pick *matsutake* mushrooms I could sell. When it was cold, I would climb into the river in my underwear and catch lots of chub with my hands for dinner. The secret was to approach them from upstream and catch them as gently as if you were caressing a woman.

Getting the all-important orders for cargo was no easy matter, and securing work was an ordeal in itself. I left the house early in the morning and worked until very late at night. When I had a big or heavy load to transport, I would ask my younger sister Kumano to help push the cart. Since we were traveling on country roads, the slightest rain or snow made things very difficult; your clothes would be filthy in five seconds flat. But she always lent a hand without a word of complaint.

Around this time, there was a craze for *Oicho-kabu*, a game played with floral playing cards, among the younger people in the village. On a trip to the Izumo Taisha grand shrine with my friend Inosuke, one of the first things I did was pick up a set of those cards. I couldn't get enough of the game. One evening, I played a game with a group of men. I have no talent for gambling, so in short order I was flat broke, having lost not only all the money I had on me, but even my leather tobacco pouch. This situation made me lightheaded and reckless. I managed to win back some money by bluffing, only to rapidly lose it all again. In no time, I had a debt of 5 yen.

"You just talk big," sneered my companions. "There's no way someone like you can get your hands on 5 yen."

I was stung by their contempt.

"It's a piddling sum. You know what? I'll pay you right now." I dashed out of the room after firing off this cutting retort. I ran across the dark paddy fields and roused Inosuke. It must have been around midnight. He stood there, dazed, sleepy-eyed, and looking thoroughly bewildered.

"I've lost at cards. Lost badly. Look, I promise I'll never gamble again, so please, lend me 5 yen."

"You've been in one of those gambling dens, have you? No way am I going to pay for that. Just leave me alone."

"But what will people think of me?"

I finally managed to wring the 5 yen out of him. Then I went back to the gambling den and, flinging the money at the men, yelled: "There. This should make you happy." Because of the promise I'd made to Inosuke, I never gambled again after that. I had learned my lesson: A person like me who does everything to extremes should never gamble.

Inosuke was like a brother to me. We had fun together almost every day, but we also had regular fights.

"I never want to see you again."

"Well, I'm glad this is the last time I'll see your ugly mug."

These were the sorts of parting shots we fired at each other. But after a day or two had gone by, one of us would always say to the other, "I'm really sorry about the other day." And the next moment we'd be deep into a discussion about girls and schemes to make money. No one else in the village had a friendship like ours.

One incident I'll never forget took place when Inosuke was twenty and I was seventeen. In those days, the Iinashi Village No. 4 Firefighting Squad was made up of members from three villages—Furukawa, Kami-ishihara, and Shimo-ishihara. The leader of the squad, who was probably around fifty, came from one of the other two villages, but Inosuke, who came from Furukawa, was foreman.

One day after a firefighting practice the squad leader organized a party, but invited only two of the three village groups, excluding Furukawa. When I heard what had happened, I confronted him. "What's going on here? Inosuke would never do anything like this, if *he* were in charge. You excluded us even though we took part in the practice the same as everybody else. You've got to take responsibility and resign."

I was young and impetuous, but I was also dealing with an important man old enough to be my father. Thinking back on it, I admire myself for having had the guts to stand up to him. In the end, the chief resigned and Inosuke took his place, carrying out his firefighting duties for several decades.

❖ ❖ ❖

One day, with no warning, my father called me in and told me I was going to be married. I'd never thought about marriage—chiefly because I didn't have anyone to get married to. I was stunned.

"The time has come for you to settle down," announced my father, who had already made up his mind. "There's no need to worry about a suitable wife, we've already found you one. She's grandpa Seizo's niece. The wedding will be next month."

Resistance was futile. What I wanted was irrelevant. You had to do what your father said in those days, so I kept my mouth shut and followed orders. Inside, I was rejoicing at the thought of having a wife while I was still in my teens.

That's how my first marriage was arranged. I was eighteen, and had lost my virginity the year before with one of the maids at a local inn. At least I was well prepared in that department! Since starting work as a hauler, I'd changed into a more dynamic person.

It wasn't until after our wedding ceremony when I removed my bride's veil that I got a proper look at her. She was childlike and petite and so modest and serious that I took an immediate liking to her. She was seventeen and her name was Tomie. Life with her was rosy. "What a wonderful thing marriage is!" I thought.

Tomie and I got on wonderfully together, but it was all over in less than three months. One day, without a word to me, my father sent her back to her parents in Arashima and arranged a divorce. Not having the faintest idea what was going on, I was a nervous wreck. It turned out that my wife had not had a period for a long time, and since there was a local legend about how the presence of such a woman would lead to the decline of the village's fortunes, my father had sent her home before word could get out.

My first marriage was thus a failure on a heroic scale. I had simply done what my parents told me. For some reason, we hadn't entered the marriage into the official family register, so I was still legally single, but we had been getting along so well that the whole thing was a massive shock. I was in a daze for quite some time.

The only reason Tomie had not had her period, I learned later, was that she was young and physically underdeveloped. When she married a second time, she gave birth to eight children! How different my life might have been if we had stayed together. Destiny works in strange ways.

✢ ✢ ✢

I will never forget this one exceptionally cold winter we had while I was working in the hauling business. So much snow fell that all the main roads in the San'in region were impassable. Everyone in Yasugi was freezing since neither horse-drawn nor hand-pulled carts could get through. At this point, I was in the wholesale charcoal business with Nojiri Rikichi, a man five years my senior. Sensing a once-in-a-lifetime opportunity, I spoke to both the men and women of the village.

"I'm prepared to pay 15 *sen* to anyone who carries two bales of charcoal down to Yasugi for me."

Townspeople would have scoffed at my proposition, but

it was an attractive offer for country folk who had nothing better to do. Like a column of ants, my team of porters trudged through the glistening white snow toward Yasugi. Each of them had two bales of charcoal on their back. When I saw how tough it was, I rushed around to get them packed lunches, while my partner did his best to find more people. For several days the snow showed no sign of letting up, and the Yasugi shipping agents told us they would take all the charcoal we could bring them. Apparently they were shipping it to Sakaiminato. Amazed at the demand, Rikichi and I wondered, in a state of disbelief, whether it was legal to make so much money.

We sold our charcoal to the wholesalers for between 3 and 5 yen a bale. This was the first time I had hired other people for a job, and my partner and I made about 250 yen each. Not only had I made a killing, I had also earned myself something of a reputation.

Success was intoxicating. Although I tried my best to be serious, I kept grinning and couldn't stop preening in front of my family. I was convinced I had a god-given talent for business. This was my first experience of how much fun making money can be.

With the money that we had made, Rikichi and I enjoyed the first *sukiyaki* of our lives and had some fun with geishas. We summoned them to Hirose for eating, drinking, and making merry. I was in heaven—this was the high point of my teenage years.

The trouble is that whenever people make money, it goes to their heads and temptation comes knocking. That's when you see what you're really made of. When you've got money for the first time in your life, your judgment tends to go haywire.

One day, a man came into town. Although he had been declared legally incompetent to conduct business, he was such a mover and a shaker that everyone addressed him as "boss."

"Start delivering charcoal to Osaka and you'll make even

more money, son," was his advice. "How 'bout going into business with me? I'll take charge of the stuff when it gets to the city and take things from there."

As far as I was concerned, he had made so much money as a rice trader that he'd become a local celebrity. I jumped at the chance to expand my business. I dispatched one wagonload of charcoal to Osaka, as the man had advised. I was overjoyed at the thought of doing business with the big city wholesalers. And the profits from this first deal did not disappoint. I was over the moon and saw myself as a great entrepreneur.

Then he proposed an even more tempting way to make money.

"Truth is, sonny, I've got me a silver mine over in Ueda. Trouble is, our capital ran out when we were about to break through to the seam, and nothing's progressed since. Just need to dig a tiny bit more and we'll be as rich as Croesus. If I bring you in as a managing partner, will you furnish me with some capital?"

He'd let me make some money from our first deal so that I would trust him, and I fell for his proposal. Abandoning the charcoal business, which I'd been in for years, I went into mining. I quite fancy becoming a mining magnate, I thought to myself, eagerly counting my financial chickens before they were hatched. My avarice was out of control.

Of course, my expectations were completely unrealistic. While veins of silver and copper did seem to exist around there, we never got to them no matter how far we extended the horizontal and vertical shafts we had dug. In no time my capital was exhausted. Used to buy machinery and pay wages, my money evaporated like so much water.

It was a mess. Not only did I lose all that I had earned, but I also burned through our modest family inheritance. My father was furious.

"How dare you help yourself to the money that our

ancestors left us!" He was terrifying. There was nothing I could say. I had been too trusting—pitifully so—and all I could do was say that I was sorry.

In the midst of all this, my grandfather encouraged me and gave me advice. "You must never get too greedy. Get too greedy and something's bound to go wrong. Having enough money to buy the ordinary, everyday things you need should be enough for anybody. Really the worst thing is that you caused other people trouble."

At that moment, my grandfather seemed almost godlike to me. The thought that someone who wasn't even a blood relative could be so kind made me so happy that I cried.

Some time before my disastrous foray into mining, one of my relatives had run off one night owing twenty sacks of rice in annual tribute to his landlord. My family had stepped in and paid the tribute for him—we bought fifteen sacks and borrowed for the other five—and the landlord told us we could rent the fields he had abandoned. My father was a farmer through and through and working in the fields was his greatest pleasure in life. My antics must have seemed wild and foolish to him, as he refused to talk to me for a long time.

The shock had a lasting effect on me. The stuffing had been knocked out of me. I drifted along and couldn't put my heart into anything.

The tryouts for joining the army were coming around soon, and I decided to become a soldier as a means of making a fresh start. From what I'd heard, no one from our village had ever become a private first class. I swore to myself that I would only come back to the village after achieving that coveted rank.

In the autumn of 1919 I turned twenty. Even my beloved countryside seemed to be giving me the cold shoulder. The mighty and ever-looming Mount Daisen felt remoter than ever. Poverty was eating me alive.

From Military Service to a Start in Business

I have lived through four different eras: Meiji, Taisho, Showa, and Heisei. By the time a man has reached my age, he's usually experienced war in some form or other, and my life seems to have been almost nothing but wars, with the Russo-Japanese War, World War I, the Manchurian Incident, the Second Sino-Japanese War, and World War II, following one after the other. There were brief periods along the way when the military machine took a rest, but the majority of Japanese ended up exposed to the horrors of war, losing their loved ones and being plunged into poverty. The sorrows and sufferings of the soldiers who were sent to the frontlines were particularly grim. We must never have another war, whatever the reason.

I did a single stint in the military as a conscript in Japan for two years and was lucky enough never to be called up for wartime service. But the boys a year ahead of me at school were eligible for the draft, and many I knew never made it back home. In war, one's will counts for nothing.

My two years in the military were one of the most important experiences of my life. I joined the 63rd Matsue Infantry Regiment as a first-grade conscript on December 1, 1919, the year after World War I ended. As part of the enlistment process, I went down to the local government office for a briefing on the military test, and—I'm ashamed to say—it was there that I first learned my own date of birth. "Don't know your own birthday! That's just not good enough," the official chided me. My birthday had never struck me as something worth remembering, but I made a point of memorizing it after this experience.

The 63rd Infantry was stationed south of Matsue in a hilly region called Koshibara. The regiment was made up of three battalions—No. 1 Battalion, No. 2 Battalion, and No. 3 Battalion—each of which was in turn made up of a battalion HQ and four companies. There were five corps, numbered one to five, in each company. I was in the third battalion, tenth company, fourth corps. Each company contained about 150 men with around 30 in a corps. My rank was private second class.

Army life was highly regulated. Every day started at 5:30 A.M. with a morning wake-up call and ended with lights out at 8:30 P.M. sharp. I was a stickler for punctuality and used to getting up and going to bed early anyway, so I didn't find the soldier's life especially disagreeable. As there was no impending war and the army was in the middle of retrenching, the discipline was not as strict as I had feared.

Probably because of my determination to become a private first class, I was always very tense while in the military. I scrupulously carried out all the tasks assigned to me, whether performing drill exercises, tidying up, or doing laundry. In fact, I was so wholeheartedly committed that I never even went off base on Sundays. The truth is that I didn't have the money to go out even if I had wanted to. And after the trouble I'd caused my family with my disastrous business venture, I could hardly expect them to send me money or give me an allowance.

When everyone else had gone, I wouldn't just clean my own stuff, but I would launder the loincloths, polish the shoes, and tidy the rooms of the corps leaders. On meal duty, we were under orders to dish out equal portions to everyone, but I would always discreetly serve the corps leaders a little more. Taking care not to be seen by the night watchman, I used to change into my uniform inside my futon so I could be the first to leap out of bed fully dressed as the bugle sounded. Before roll call, I would fold up the futons of the privates first class as well as my own. And when we were on maneuvers, I would strap on everyone's canteens, from the corps leader down, and head off by myself to fetch water from the bottom of the valley. As usual I was hopeless at the intellectual side of things, so I took on all the tasks that no one else wanted to do. In other words, I became a total suck-up.

Bribery was the most normal route to promotion, but I

didn't have the money for that. Playing the part of attentive wife and housekeeper to my superiors struck me as my best strategy. Not surprisingly, this tactic made me very popular with the officers. They all knew I was aiming for a double promotion to private first class and made me their pet, even awarding me three prizes for diligence. Normally, corps leaders will do all they can to make sure that their own corps is the one to turn out first class privates, but my sucking-up strategy worked so well that all of them recommended me and I was promoted to PFC a year after joining up. This exceptional promotion boosted my confidence and proved to me that anything is possible, if you put your heart and soul into it—a philosophy that I've maintained ever since. If you slog your guts out, people will notice. My determination to impress led to results. The perseverance I learned in the army made me even more dynamic than I had been before.

While in the army, I got a stipend of 8 *sen* every ten days, which I spent on everyday necessities and bean-jam buns. Having developed an acute sense of the value of money, I was never tempted to waste it. I stayed quietly in the barracks without even applying for permission to go off base.

One day, around six months after I had joined up, I received a letter. It was from my grandfather. He had written me a brief note telling me to take good care of my health and had enclosed the huge sum of 50 *sen*. Tears sprang to my eyes when I realized that he must have cut back on his beloved sake to save so much. My grandfather—and my mother—never stopped thinking of me.

Once, we were set to go on a training march due to pass quite near my house. Planning to drop in for lunch, I sent advance word to my parents. I'm not sure why, but the order came down and the march was unexpectedly cancelled. I was still thoroughly miserable a few days later when my mother appeared at the regiment on visiting day. She had brought a bottle of beer and an armful of rice cakes to cheer me up and had walked all the way over the Komagae Pass because she couldn't afford the fare from Arashima to Matsue.

The mountain road was full of ups and downs and used by so few people that it was more of an animal trail than a proper road. I knew it was a hard journey that would take a woman half a day. And sure enough, my mother had gotten up before sunrise to make it to the regiment just before midday. The weather was hot and humid and her face was deeply flushed. I was so overcome with emotion that I couldn't say a word. She smiled at me, and I felt as though I had been smiled on by Kannon, goddess of mercy.

❖ ❖ ❖

One of our army drills was practicing descents. Even as a child, I had never been much of a sportsman. I was hopeless at any kind of outdoor drill, but descents was the one I hated the most. I was terrified of heights, and standing on a platform even a foot off the ground was enough to make me go weak in the knees. When I saw the other men happily running up and leaping off the twelve-step tower, I got goose bumps. I would let them all go ahead of me in a futile effort to put off the inevitable.

Finally, resigned to my fate, I would pull myself fearfully up the stairs. It was as harrowing as mounting the scaffold. When I finally made it to the top, my knees would shake, and I would crash to the floor.

"Hey, Adachi. What are you doing wasting time up there? Jump! Now!"

The corps leader could yell at me all he liked—nothing changed the fact that my legs had turned to jelly and I couldn't move. I was in a cold sweat, my knees trembling, my heart pounding.

"I'm begging you, sir," I would plead. "Can't you let me

off just this once?" Naturally, they never paid the slightest attention to my whining.

"You damn fool! Call yourself a man, Adachi? Got any balls, have you?"

What he said made no difference. Heights and earthquakes are the two things that terrify me. "Mommy, help me!" I silently prayed as I shut my eyes and launched myself into the void. Then I landed so heavily on the base of my spine that I had to be carted off to sick bay—pathetic!

Now for my second disaster story. One morning, around twenty of us reported to the parade ground for kit inspection. We all stood rigidly upright. As a private first class, I was at the head of the first row, with an intensely serious expression on my face.

"Atten-*shun!*"

We were all quite nervous at the thought of being inspected by this terrifying commandant. Sure enough, his mustachioed and stern visage was the picture of stern authority. But somehow the way his tightly pursed lips turned down at the corners reminded me of the painted-on face of a roly-poly *daruma* doll. No sooner had the thought occurred to me, than a laugh rose to my lips. I tried everything I could to suppress it—crossing my legs, biting my lip—but nothing worked. I snickered aloud and the cat was out of the bag.

"You bloody fool!"

The commandant was furious. He charged over and gave me such an almighty shove that I did a backward somersault. You'd think that would have cured my laughter, but I just kept right at it. My eyes were streaming tears and my stomach was cramping, as the commandant grew more and more rabid. He had forgotten all about the kit inspection. In the end, I was marched off to the detention barracks and given a thorough beating, which probably rearranged my features a little for the better! Word of what had happened was passed on to my superior officers, and the company commander summoned me to his room that evening. "There is such a thing as being *too* relaxed. You're an embarrassment to the regiment." He gave me an earful, but at least he didn't hit me.

That's the way I am—I can't stop once I've started to laugh or cry. My emotions have always been too strong. I have mellowed a little with age and can keep a better grip on myself. Anyway, this was the biggest disaster brought about by my runaway emotions. Even

Me in uniform, at the time I joined the 63rd Matsue Infantry Regiment.

now, whenever I try to tell this story, I end up laughing so much that I can't get a word out. "People never change" goes the saying, and I certainly never seem to improve.

In April of my second year in the military, I was made responsible for the new recruits. Later I was put in charge of weapons and of shooting practice. My second year was pretty restful, and I almost never had to take part in field maneuvers. The instant I made private first class, I became a complete layabout, cutting corners wherever I could. Frankly, I was amazed at the speed of my transformation. There's not much I can say in my defense.

My promotion to private first class meant that my stipend increased to 15 *sen*. Since I was a little better-off than before, I got a permit to leave the base and hurried to the local red-light district. The mere sight and fragrance of the girl I chose there were enough to make me happy. I thought it would spoil things if we rushed ourselves, so instead we embarked on a long discussion about our hometowns, our families, even our childhood experiences, until, before we knew it, time was up. There was the option of paying for extra time, but naturally I didn't have the money. All we had time for was to clasp each other's hands and say goodbye.

"I really enjoyed today," the girl said as I was leaving. "Do come again, won't you? We can talk some more." This was like rubbing salt in the wound. In the end I didn't manage to do what I'd been dreaming of for such a long time and gloomily plodded back through the town to the barracks. I was so disgruntled that I couldn't get a wink of sleep that night. I felt like such a boob!

✧ ✧ ✧

By the time I had only a month left in my service, I couldn't concentrate on my lessons. As I pored over the numbers, the only thought on my mind was the day of my discharge. The last maneuvers I took part in were held around this time, and for once, I was serious about them. We were finally presented with our rice rations at 11 P.M. after the maneuvers had ended. We were all hungry and exhausted, and found the idea of cooking rice so late at night thoroughly depressing.

"Just leave this to me," I said, and started haggling with a black-market bread seller, eventually trading our rice for bean-jam buns. Everyone was pleased. As usual, I was right on target when it came to guessing what other people wanted. Of course, a few buns were discreetly slipped my way in recognition of my trouble. In those days, food was hard to come by, and we were always hungry. It's rather embarrassing, but I gobbled down so many of them that I got diarrhea.

During maneuvers on the parade ground the next day, I broke out in a cold sweat, and as soon as we were ordered to take a five-minute break, I squatted and squirted right there, in plain view of everybody. "Necessity knows no law," would be the *mot juste* for this situation.

My last day of leave before my final discharge came around. This time I decided to spend the night in Hirata because I was friendly with a geisha there. I had learned my lesson from the recent fiasco, and spent a wonderful night, delighting in my first physical contact with a woman in two years. I was surprised and touched when the geisha paid for everything out of her own pocket. "Maybe I do have a smidgen of charm after all," I thought to myself conceitedly.

✤ ✤ ✤

It was the end of November 1921, and my two-year tour of duty had come safely to an end. Elated, I headed home after buying some presents for my family and a commemorative cup. As my village's first-ever private first class, I returned in triumph. The village even flew a flag to welcome me home, but in little more than a week I had made up my mind to light out for Osaka to see what my uncle could do for me there.

"You could at least celebrate the New Year at home with us," grumbled my family, trying to stop me. But I had decided while I was in the army that I wanted to get a job as soon as possible to put my parents' minds at ease.

To cover the costs of the trip to Osaka, I cut down some thick-stemmed bamboo and sold it to a bamboo workshop for almost 4 yen. In those days, the train fare to Osaka from Arashima in third class was a little more than 3 yen.

A piercingly cold December wind was blowing the night I left. With my wicker trunk on my back, I walked at a brisk trot along the pitch-dark road to Arashima Station with my mother.

It was nearly 4 miles past rice paddies and mountains. On the way, we passed Iinashi Elementary School, my alma mater, and though I wasn't the least bit fond of it, I couldn't help feeling nostalgic. Perhaps I was emotionally charged as I had recently finished my military service.

In those days, there was only one through train to Osaka in the morning, and another in the evening. I was going to catch the night train, which left at 11 P.M. Although I told my mother that there was no need for her to come and see me off as it was dangerous and I was no longer a child, she paid no attention.

"Don't be too naive and trusting," she advised me as we walked. "On the other hand, if you're too crafty and cunning, you won't make any friends either. There are all sorts of people in the big city, not all of them nice, so you'd best be careful." She was genuinely worried. I was already twenty-two, but from her point of view I was still as helpless as a babe in arms. Maybe my failure in the mining venture made her worry overmuch about me. Or perhaps it was my character, mercenary and scatterbrained at the same time, that aroused her concern.

My uncle in Osaka was working as a cook for a small catering shop in Minami Honmachi 2-chome in Higashi-ku. By coincidence, this was very close to the Maruzen Building that would later become my base of operations in Osaka.

I worked there for about a month and a half from the start of the new year, while living on the premises. I wasn't officially employed, just helping out while learning the ropes. I received meals rather than a salary for my labor. And when I quit, all I got was a small hand towel. I had zero interest in catering, but I worked unstintingly hard because I liked being busy. My efforts caught the attention of the owner, a Mr. Nakao.

"There's no point in your staying on here," he told me and introduced me to a wholesaler of charcoal and charcoal briquettes. This new job was to be my first ever business apprenticeship.

The shop was near the east gate of the temple Tenno-ji. There were seven or eight apprentices. Several of them were younger than me, but since I was the most recent recruit, I was always the last in line to eat or get a bath.

We were fed rice porridge with miso soup and pickles. To reduce the amount of cleaning that needed to be done, we were not allowed to eat on the tatami, and so we ate on the cement floor. As our job was handling charcoal, the bathroom would soon get filthy. Cleaning it was a Herculean task.

My job was to come up with new ways to earn money, and the boss liked me for being a hard worker. Charcoal briquettes that would catch fire as soon as you put a match to them had recently begun to be sold, and our sales were outpacing everyone else's. I won lots of regular customers by doing little favors for people like helping the maid at an inn that bought from us move their brazier. I was putting the experience of making people feel good I'd gained in the army to good use, which enabled me to sell some on the side.

In the meantime, I began to understand how lucrative this business was. As the briquettes are simply combustible balls made from charcoal, powdered coal, and a little glue, they cost next to nothing to make. Nonetheless, in an age when there was little in the way of mechanical heating, they were a necessity, meaning that there was huge demand for them. So much so, in fact, that dealers were happy to have them delivered before they had even dried properly. It was a business with sky-high profit margins—provided, of course, you could put up with being dirty all the time.

It occurred to me that this was my chance! I asked one of the briquette makers how I could get my hands on the necessary raw materials and to explain the manufacturing process. I planned to start making briquettes in three months time. I had a word with Mr. Nakao, the owner of the catering business, and he was champing at the bit.

"Sounds good to me," he said. "Handily enough, I happen to have a factory near Ikuno Junior High School that is empty right now. How about I provide the capital and the factory and we split any profits fifty-fifty?" And so everything was agreed. Mr. Nakao was rich and generous, and he had a keen nose for an opportunity. This was how I began manufacturing charcoal briquettes. Since I was both a manufacturer and a salesman, I was very busy visiting all the different wholesalers I dealt with.

One day, when I was walking along the street looking at a fruit seller's shop, I noticed a beggar striding toward me. His shirt was too big for him, his pants were baggy, and his face was totally black. "What a filthy, dirty fellow," I thought to myself absentmindedly, then noticed that he was looking at me with the same expression of distaste. "I know I've seen that face somewhere before," I thought, then stopped short in my tracks. I was looking at my own reflection in a mirror! I was dumbstruck. "Making money ain't easy," I thought with a sigh. I never gave a second thought to what I looked like in those days. When I was working I became black all over; my nose, my fingernails, the nape of my neck, everywhere was caked with soot.

Around the same time, an advertising billboard displaying a list of the country's millionaires caught my eye as I was walking through the city. Glancing at it offhandedly, I notice that mixed in with the famous corporate conglomerates, such as Mitsui, Sumitomo, and Mitsubishi, were a couple of the big San'in families—Tanabe Choemon and Itaguchi Heibei. I felt immensely proud of my home region at the sight.

My briquette business was every bit as profitable as I'd hoped it would be. A big freeze the year before had caused a shortage of briquettes, and the wholesalers were all placing big orders that summer to avoid being caught short again. It made more sense for me to sell as much as I could now rather than wait for the weather to turn cold. I was impatient for my briquettes to dry and sold them at a furious pace. Profits rose to an amazing 1,800 yen, meaning that Mr. Nakao and I ended up with 900 yen each. This was equivalent to 150 bales of rice.

I was thrilled at our unexpected success. Eager to report back to my parents as soon as possible, I headed back to my hometown, self-satisfaction glistening from every pore of my face.

The folks at home had been awaiting my return no less eagerly. The joy of my parents and grandparents knew no bounds. My mother, bursting with happiness, urged me to get married.

"You've done so well," she said. "Why not forget all about going back to Osaka? Hurry up and find yourself a nice wife here and father some grandchildren for me." Having had so little to do with women for so long, I didn't think it a bad idea. And that was why, in 1922, I decided to marry Ishii Matsuyo, a local girl and one of my friends.

Although I had solemnly promised Mr. Nakao that I would continue working with him in Osaka, our relationship now came to an end. I sent him presents on a couple of occasions, but we gradually drifted apart. Several years later I went to the building where the caterer's had been, but the place was shut and no one in the area knew where Mr. Nakao had gone. I went to the former site of the briquette factory, but the whole district had been rebuilt and there was no trace of it. When I had known him, he had a couple of still very young children. Years afterward every time I heard the name Nakao, I would ask about the man's age and appearance to see if it was the person I had once known, but time after time it turned out to be someone else. I have never forgotten Mr. Nakao. He was one of my greatest benefactors, and I still bitterly regret that I had failed in my duty toward him. By now he himself must have passed on, but I would still like to track down his children.

❖ ❖ ❖

A new problem broke out when my family and I found ourselves embroiled in an argument with our landlord about our right to use the rice paddies of one of our relatives who had run off. The landlord had been happy to take the twenty bales of rice we gave him, including five we had bought on credit, but then broke his promise and rented the paddies out to someone else instead of letting us use them as agreed. When my parents told me what was going on, I rushed over to negotiate with him. "Give us back our twenty bales of rice if you're not going to let us use the rice paddies," I said. But the landlord wouldn't so much as give me the time of day. "If you don't give us back our twenty bales of rice, then I'll stay here and I won't budge, come hell or high water," I yelled over the wall of his mistress's house. The head clerk from his main residence came to meet me. I stood there for hours, but the landlord simply refused to open the door. My blood was boiling. "Right," I exploded. "Then I'm going to prosecute."

The next day, the local police chief came around to our house.

"So, Osaka turned you into a commie, did it? Damn disgrace. Come with me to the station."

He hauled me off, and, believe it or not, I was threatened with prosecution. I was confident there was no way I'd lose if the dispute went to trial, but pressured by local opinion, I eventually accepted that discretion was the better part of valor. In those days, the landlords were hand in glove with the authorities, and they banded together to grind small tenant farmers down. There was nothing I could do, but I was so angry that I couldn't sleep for weeks.

Two years later, the tenant farmers' protest erupted. Starting in Nogi, the tenants started establishing associations and were soon followed by other prefectures. These actions led to a significant improvement in the relationship between landlords and tenants, as the old feudal elements were done away with. Rents were permanently reduced to fairer levels. These were reforms whose time had come.

I thought this run-in with the landlord would shock my father, since he was a born and bred farmer, but he very much took the whole thing in stride. This was due in part to his unexpected (and largely accidental) success in a new venture, the cultivation of eggplant seedlings, from which he made an amazing 120 yen. I was astounded and forced to revise my opinion of him. This man can really do it, I thought.

My marriage seemed like a good enough time for it, so, capitalizing on my experience, I founded my first company, the San'in Charcoal Briquette Joint Stock Company. I used an old row house building in Hirose as our factory. I had already tasted success in Osaka, and now I was aiming to again. My partner was Nojiri Rikichi; we'd made a killing together by hiring people to transport charcoal to Yasugi during that great snowstorm several years prior. Since sawdust was one of the ingredients of briquettes, we even negotiated with a lumber factory. I was in charge of sales; Nojiri of deliveries.

But things weren't easy. Demand was slow compared to Osaka and we ended doing lots of work for little reward. After a year, I decided to go back to rice brokering, a business I had been in earlier. This has always been my way: The instant I felt something wasn't working out, I would pack up my stall and move on. "Quick to decide, quick to act" is my motto. This was how I ended up shuttering the first local company I founded all too soon.

The rice-brokering business went well. At the time, a bale of rice sold for 6 yen. I had access to even the biggest landholders. To get orders, I would show samples from the farmers and landlords to all the local rice and grain merchants. My biggest clients were the Yamanaga Rice Mill in Yasugi and the Fujii and Kuwabara rice mills in Hirose. (Fujii Toshiro, from the Fujii Rice Mill family, is the current president of San'in Broadcasting Company.) They paid me 10 *sen* per bale in commission. In the off-season from October to March, I would bicycle around Arashima and Yasugi near where I lived, but from April to October I would cycle to Arashima Station and take the train to Matsue. After securing an order, five bales here, ten bales there, I would plan to deliver the rice the next day. Every other day, my friend Inosuke would make the deliveries to our clients by horse cart.

The clients gradually started trusting our company. I didn't just focus on the commercial side of things—buying the rice a little cheaper from the farmer, getting a slightly higher commission from the rice dealer—but made a point of chatting with the customers and asking them how they were. We won more and more regular accounts, and business was humming along. I had already tried my hand at a variety of businesses, but rice brokering seemed to suit me best.

I was keen to expand. While running my rice-brokering business, I had opened a general store called Adachi's on the road near Saginoyu Onsen. I had even managed to persuade my parents to get out of farming and help with the shop instead. Trade was good. My father suddenly discovered that he had a knack for business. He had somehow found out that glutinous rice, *mochigome,* was in short supply, so I, with my usual trader mentality, announced that we ought to buy plenty of it while we could, as the price was sure to rise. Sure enough, a general shortage of glutinous rice followed, and the price went through the roof.

When I suggested that perhaps the time to sell had come, my father roared at me. "No way, it's still too early." I was awestruck. This sixth sense for business had been sleeping inside my father all along. Perhaps I had inherited my nose for a deal from him after all.

While dealing in rice on one hand, I was also gratified by the good reputation that the store was earning for itself. Convinced that the business would never really take off unless we had a wider selection of stuff, I bought a load of goods. The plan, however, backfired. As the inventory grew bloated, I started experiencing financial problems, and my main creditor ended up serving me with an order of seizure, attaching red tags to all the better goods in the shop. My wife and I put up the shutters, pulled the curtains closed, and didn't get a wink of sleep for twelve days. Too ashamed to go outside during the daytime, we waited for night to fall before slipping out. Never in my life has time dragged by so slowly.

I've always liked to tackle new things and I've no aversion to changing the sort of work I do. Wham! An idea comes to me in a flash of inspiration. Bam! I move straight into action. Since pulling a handcart as a teenager, I had seen several businesses through cycles of success and failure. If any business I was in did well, I'd immediately try to expand it; this would then lead to failure and my moving on to something new. Naturally, trying one's luck in a new field was risky, but it made the pleasure of succeeding that much sweeter. I have always liked to dream big; business on a small scale simply didn't interest me.

Nonetheless, what with my mining failure and now this, I was having a run of bad luck with my local efforts. Suspecting that my name, Yoshimoto, might be the cause of this, I consulted a fortune-teller who specialized in the analysis of names. On his advice, I changed my name to Zenko, which means something like "good deeds." The two characters that make up the name—善行—can also be read as "Masayasu," but I opted for the Chinese-style reading as I thought Zenko sounded better. I know they're only being polite, but I love it when people tell me that it's a rare and lucky name.

Putting my mother and father in charge of the shop, I set off again for Osaka to replenish our stock. I struck up a relationship with a receiver through whom I was able to acquire clothes cheaply and in large quantities from bankrupt firms and cash-strapped shops. I sold most of the clothes wholesale to shops in Hirose and Yasugi and the rest from our own shop at retail.

✦ ✦ ✦

My life of shuttling between Yasugi and Osaka as a broker continued for some years. During this time I met a man called Shinoda Yaichiro in Osaka. About five years older than me, he had come to Osaka when the draper's business he'd been running for quite a while in Gifu had gone belly-up. When I first met him he didn't have a shop of his own, so he started wholesaling knitted goods in a so-so place I'd introduced him to in the Fukushima area of the city. At the time he had no capital, and so he would come by to borrow money almost on a daily basis. Gradually his business made it onto a solid footing, and our relationship became more of a give-and-take affair.

Unlike me, Shinoda was very precise about his accounts, but he was also a big-hearted man. We were very similar and got along like a house on fire. When there was money to be made, we would each make concessions to make sure we both got a fair share. If any of the firms we did business with went bankrupt, he'd say to the company head, "Look, there's no need for you to pay me what you owe me." Then he would give the man a pat on the back and say, "More important, if you need any goods to sell, just say the word and I'll send them right over. I want you to make a lot of money." He was always sympathetic.

I suppose he was unable to ignore people's pain and suffering because he had once suffered through bankruptcy and was a warm-hearted man. He became my dearest friend, and we collaborated on a whole range of businesses both before and after the war. Our relationship lasted about forty years.

Years later, when Shinoda was on his deathbed, I got a phone call in the middle of the night and rushed over to see him. Everyone else there was his immediate family. When he saw me, his eyes opened wide—it was clear he wanted to speak to me, though he was unable to utter a sound. I began to cry. We gazed into one another's eyes, then he clasped my hand tight and breathed his last. I will never forget the look in his eyes. He was my partner in the true sense of the word, and a lifelong friend in both the business and private spheres of my life. Getting to know him greatly expanded not just my range of business contacts but the goods I handled, as well as the breadth of my activities.

My Smile:
My Life Partner

Most people are not meant to live their lives alone. Both at home and in the workplace, wonderful friends fill our lives with joy, making work fun and leisure a pleasure. Who you meet and become friends with has a direct influence on the course of your life. People who fail to see how crucial the people they meet are, who fail to seize the chances they are presented with, are wasting their lives.

Making a good first impression, and I'm not recommending sycophancy, is an important skill and shapes your encounters with other people. I worked hard to ensure that I'd always be ready to meet and make friends with people. And what was my trump card? A smile.

There are two kinds of smiles: the one we're born with and the one we have as adults. We all have a natural, innate smile and an acquired smile. Most of us are happy to see the innocent smile of a child, but many of us probably detect something forced and objectionable in the smiles of adults. I think that a degree of suspicion and caution reveals itself in our smiles without our awareness. When people are taking stock of one another, it's no surprise that their smiles become stiff and forced, but a smile that looks phony and insincere is hardly going to put someone in a good mood.

I took the business of smiling seriously and diligently practiced my smile from a young age. I would look at myself in the mirror every day, turning to the left and then the right, pulling up the corners of my mouth, relaxing them, and trying to radiate cheerfulness. It was like an exercise routine for my face. I kept up this routine until very recently, but have given up now that I seem to have reached an age when everyone regards me as a good-natured old duffer anyway! At my age, practicing probably wouldn't lead to any improvement anyway.

"By the time you're forty, you have the face you deserve" goes the proverb. I think working on your smile should be a big part of that. Even now I still pester my family and colleagues about how they should work on their smiles, though I don't think they pay much attention. "Uh-oh, here we go again," they think and slip off. How mortifying!

I talk a lot about smiling because it was responsible for my having the good fortune to meet so many people. The positive impression my smile created when I first met people enabled me to make the acquaintance of many capable men like Shinoda Yaichiro, an Osaka businessman and my dearest friend.

I am not naïve enough to think that a nice smile is enough to make people trust you, but I do believe that it can soften up an acquaintance and dispose him favorably toward you. After all, no one dislikes being smiled at! And having a lovely smile is the first step for any woman who aspires to be beautiful.

When I set up the general store in my hometown a little before meeting Shinoda in Osaka, I became acquainted with Hata Gishiro, who owned a wholesale fishmonger's in Matsue. I was sure that my smile had played an important role in bringing us together. Sure enough, a few days after we'd gotten to know one another, he told me I had a "nice face." I choose to think he was referring to my smile.

Mr. Hata noticed how I went about my work and would give me snippets of advice. Thanks to his behind-the-scenes help I was able to hand the management of the store over to my parents and head for Osaka. He was the first powerful patron I had in my local area.

Once I moved to Osaka, the number of people I did business with gradually increased. For several years, I shuttled to and fro between Osaka and my hometown. Going to Osaka was like a "trip to market" for me, but once my business had started to prosper, I decided to try and settle down at home for a second time. I drifted between Hirose and Yasugi for a while, moving from one appealing location to another.

In 1927, I got myself a first-class property in Yonago and

established San'in Textile Wholesalers. I called it a wholesaler, but really it was a general store that sold retail as well. After coming up with all sorts of potential names, we finally called the place Mikiriya—it means "sell at a bargain price"—since I was a big believer in selling things cheaply. News of the shop spread rapidly by word of mouth and customers came pouring in from all the nearby towns and villages. In a way Mikiriya was a forerunner of the discount stores that are so popular nowadays. We would sell some products at a loss, sometimes for half of or less than half of the normal price, simply to lure people into the store.

I told Mr. Hata that the business represented a one-in-a-million chance. With him as my guarantor, three investors put up 100 yen each for a total of 300. I wanted to increase the scale of my business but could not do so without a war chest. Mr. Hata promised to give me his full cooperation as he also believed that there was nothing better than doing business on a big scale.

My mother's reaction to the plan was very different. "Please don't get into debt," she implored me. "That's all I ask of you."

My mother's fear of my failing was obviously stronger than her faith I would succeed. The debacle with the silver mine had clearly been a big shock. I tried to tell her that things would not end up the same way this time and that she didn't need to worry, but she remained anxious.

At this same time an acquaintance in Osaka approached me with a proposal. "I've heard about a shop that's having cash-flow problems. They want to sell off their entire stock for 800 yen. Are you interested?" Eight hundred yen seemed way beyond my reach, but his talk of mountains of clothes had piqued my interest. I headed straight for Osaka.

There I found almost thirty large garment boxes crammed with all sorts of clothing—shirts, underwear, children's clothes, work clothes. The moment I saw it all, I knew it was the chance for me to make a killing.

"I'll leave the 300 yen I've got on me here with you now," I said. "The remaining 500 yen I'll get to you in a day or two. Get ready to ship the stuff over to me, okay?"

On the train home I racked my brains trying to think of a way to scrape together the outstanding 500 yen, but inspiration didn't come. Approaching Mr. Hata yet again would have been embarrassing. "Oh, I've really gone and put my foot in it now," I was thinking as we pulled into Arashima Station.

As I got off the train, I glimpsed the name Arashima on a sign. Suddenly, I remembered that my cousin and Kumano, my younger sister, who lived near the station, had some money of their own. They also had some standing and influence in the community, so it might be well worth my while to have a word with them. Who knows, with all the money they had, they might be interested.

I went to see my cousin and got straight to the point. "I promise to make it worth your while. How about it?" A brisk and decisive man, he expressed his interest, spoke to several other people, and mustered up 500 yen in no time. I went home, but no sooner did I tell my mother what I'd done than she again burst into tears.

"My boy squandered 300 yen," she wailed. "And not content with that, now he's going to lose another 500!" I had no idea how to comfort her. The more detail I went into, the more she sobbed. I was at my wits' end.

Shrugging off my mother's efforts to hold me back, the next day I set off for Osaka with my cousin to finalize the deal. For some reason, I was unshakably confident that I would turn a profit. And sure enough, the transaction went off even better than I'd anticipated. There was such a quantity and variety of clothing, and it was all so cheap, that an endless stream of customers came to the Hirose shop where I had rented a space—we

My wife, Matsuyo, and I. Together we had two children.

made our money back in only a week, right before the Old Lunar New Year.

True to my word, I repaid my backers interest above and beyond the principal, thus raising my credit another notch in my circle. This experience taught me that if you make money for people once, they'll be happy to lend you what you need next time around. Afterward I gradually expanded my business by borrowing money whenever I needed to. I began to think seriously about what I needed to do to earn other people's trust. Business is all about making money; turning a profit is what makes it so much fun.

I got myself a license, bought a motorbike, and started to develop my wholesale business. Making good use of my knowledge of the Osaka and Izumo dialects, I whizzed among shops in Hirose, Yasugi, and Matsue. I was to stay in Yonago for most of the next decade, building the foundation and saving the funds for my next venture. My businesses started to perform very well.

✧ ✧ ✧

Meanwhile all sorts of things were going on in my personal life. My eldest son, Tsuneo, was born in 1923, the year after I got married for the second time. My grandfather Seizo, who had been delighted at the birth of his great-grandson, died of old age in February 1929. He passed away in his sleep at the age of eighty-four. Just three days earlier, he had been well enough to sing the *yasugibushi*, a local folk song, along with the phonograph. This was the first time in my life I had lost a family member; I was heartbroken.

My second son, Tadaaki, was born in April 1931, and my grandmother Mon passed away only six months later. She was eighty. Then, only two years later, my wife, Matsuyo, died from tuberculosis (incurable in those days), leaving behind a not-yet-weaned baby. She was only twenty-eight.

This phase of my life had a unique emotional intensity because I had to deal with so many deaths and births in my family. I had spent very little time in my hometown as an adult until then, so it was all the more extraordinary that I was visited by this succession of joys and sorrows. Perhaps my sixth sense had warned me about what was going to happen.

My marriages, however, were one agony after another. My first marriage had ended with my wife and I being forcibly separated after less than three months; and in my second, I lost my wife while she was still a young woman. My business had started to prosper, and life with two very young children, despite my parents being alive and well and able to help out, was extremely inconvenient.

I was the sort of man who had always left my wife, parents, and sisters to look after the children. I had no idea how to be a proper father. "Serves you right," you might say, but I couldn't change my stripes and become a good family man overnight. My work was my life, and I wanted to create an environment where I could focus on it without distractions.

Not long after losing my second wife, I started living with a woman who had been a waitress at a restaurant called Kinmei-tei. She was two years older than me, with a daughter of almost twenty and a mother-in-law in tow. Since I was busy running my shop, it was essential for me to find a woman able to take care of my children. We were a family of six all told, including me and my two children, and had a lively existence at a place I had rented and from which I was running a general store in Hosshojimachi in Yonago.

The woman did not just take care of the children, but she also managed the shop and its accounts. Her daughter worked as a shop assistant, and her mother-in-law took care of the housework and the cooking. My children were still young, so they adjusted to their new mother pretty quickly, and I felt secure enough to turn my full attention to my work.

Then, the woman and I went to Osaka where I started a wholesale textile business from a shop I'd had my eye on in Awaza. So now I had a base in Osaka. I hired five of my relatives to help me and business went well. This was the start of a double life spent shuttling between Yonago and Osaka. Even though it might have looked thoroughly inconvenient to most people, since I've never been the sort of person to put down roots, I felt I had finally found a good rhythm for my life. I was away from home a lot, though, so it's hard to say I was a good father to my children.

Around this time Tsuneo, my eldest son, who was in the sixth grade, was due to go on a school trip. They were going to Osaka, so I got in touch with Yasuko, my youngest sister, who was living there at the time and asked her to take care of her nephew. But the trip was cancelled suddenly so I sent her a telegram that read: "Tsuneo. Trip cancelled."

That evening Yasuko rushed over from Osaka, her face as white as a sheet. "I can't believe Tsuneo's dead!"

I had no idea what she was talking about and just gawped at her, but it didn't take long to solve the mystery. Yasuko had interpreted my telegram as meaning that Tsuneo had died during his journey. As it was printed in the phonetic script *katakana*, I realized that a small error in the spacing between words had caused this misunderstanding. It was a good example of my stupidity at work. And it's certainly one episode from my hectic and irregular life that I won't be forgetting in a hurry.

I trusted the woman implicitly, but my life with her didn't last long. A few years later she ran off, taking all the money from the shop. Since I had set up her daughter with a dress-making shop and even adopted her son-in-law into my family, I was shocked at the betrayal. I ruefully wondered why I was so unlucky in love.

But that's not to say that I was blameless. I had become intimate with another of the women working at the same restaurant, and had set this other woman up in a place of her own in Yonago. Finding out about this was probably what had driven her to run away, and so it was difficult to stay angry.

My newest girlfriend also had a daughter by a former marriage. She was young and pretty. I'm a tenderhearted soul and a sucker for female charm—it's my Achilles' heel. I melt the moment I see a nice-looking girl, and I became involved with the mother in part from a desire to help her daughter. I've no shortage of stories, both good and bad, involving women.

I was still leaving my children in the care of my parents and my sister. My elder son was thirteen, and the younger only five. With regard to getting remarried, my feelings were, no thanks, at least for now. But I knew I couldn't leave my boys with my parents permanently. I also knew that my parents were keen for me to remarry, so I decided to take the plunge, hoping to prove the proverbial "third time's the charm." My bride, of course, was my new girlfriend from the restaurant. I was forty at the time, and this was to be my last marriage. My wife's name was Masako. At last I had established a framework that let me focus wholeheartedly on my work.

One year later, in 1940, my mother, who had taken such loving care of me for so long, passed away. She was sixty-two years old. I was very close to my mother, so her death was a terrible blow. In her last years, she had worked as hard as ever, taking care of her grandchildren and running a tight ship at Adachi's, the general store she had managed.

As I stood beside her casket, a host of images flashed before my eyes; my mother comforting me when I was making a scene about not wanting to go to school; her radiant smile when she walked over to see me during my time in the army; her grief-stricken expression after the failure of my mining venture.

✣ ✣ ✣

My private life was filled with a series of weddings and funerals from 1925 to 1940. At times, this made work difficult, but I managed to pull through thanks to several marvelous businessmen I got to know. Mr. Hata from Matsue and Mr. Shinoda from Osaka head that list, but there is a third man, Matsumoto Shigeru, whom I also met in Osaka. We were polar opposites, which, oddly enough, put us on the same wavelength.

I first got to know Matsumoto before the war when I happened to drop into his shop to buy myself a pair of socks. He had been manufacturing socks in Banshu in Hyogo Prefecture until his twenties, but relocated to Senba in Osaka eager to make his mark in business. About ten years my junior, he had enormous nerve, not to mention a memory for and ability to do sums that made his brain like a comprehensive ledger. When we first got to know each other, I loaned him money and acted as his guarantor. He started out in textiles, but later moved into real estate on my advice, becoming hugely wealthy thanks to property he owned in Suita and other parts of Osaka.

We were opposites, but for some reason we got along fantastically well. I was hasty and impatient, while he was thick-skinned and laid-back. Whether buying stocks or betting on horses, he was a keen gambler. He certainly worked hard, but he took the business of having fun more seriously than anything else. He couldn't have cared less about punctuality; he was quite happy to keep someone waiting for an entire hour. I told him thousands of times that I didn't mind any of his other habits, but that I wanted him to make an effort to be punctual, and eventually he got in the habit of arriving for meetings with me—and me alone—on time. He was a lone wolf who did not much like joining forces with other people, so I didn't get that many opportunities to work with him. More than anything else, he was a great friend with whom I had a lot of fun.

He was an extraordinary man. He would calmly practice his *nagauta* kabuki songs upstairs in his home while a horde of debt collectors milled around on the floor below. He was a cool customer and must have had nerves of steel. And he never bragged about himself, nor did he ever complain about anything.

Although he seemed to never get upset, he was actually very sensitive and was hugely attentive to other people. Whenever I was even mildly sick, he would drop whatever he had been doing and run to my bedside with a mountain of gifts. Knowing how obsessive I was about my work, he was always good-naturedly suggesting we go for dinner at some nice restaurant he'd discovered or take a relaxing jaunt to a hot spring.

Several years ago I came down with the flu, and it wasn't showing any signs of going away. "You've got to be careful. You really don't want this to develop into pneumonia," Matsumoto advised me. "I've taken a special room for you in the hospital of a friend of mine. Check yourself in as soon as you can." When I got to the hospital I was astounded. Matsumoto had provided everything—traditional Chinese medicine, antibiotics, even hair growth tonic! Although I was grateful for his concern, I couldn't help feeling that he had slightly overdone it. On the surface, he looked like a rogue, but he was a very sensitive man.

Once more than ten years ago while I was in Osaka, I got

a call from Matsumoto out of the blue announcing that he was on his way over to see me. I had a feeling in my bones that he had been on a trip somewhere in Japan and had brought back either *matsutake* mushrooms or eel as a present for me. Sure enough, as soon as he arrived he whipped out some eel.

"Matsumoto-san," I said, "my sixth sense told me you'd be bringing me eel or *matsutake* mushrooms, and I hit the nail on the head. I'm delighted with the present, but the truth is I need to raise about 300 million yen and I just can't get the last 70 million together. Right now, you look to me like a man who's got more money than he knows what to do with. I suspect I could get it from you easily enough. What do you say? You come to give me a present and I demand a loan on top. If nothing else, it'll make a nice anecdote for you to tell."

"Well, you're right, I do have the money. Let's do the deal. I'll just go and fetch it."

With such a large sum of money involved, this story may sound like tasteless bragging, but it shows how close we were.

Come to think of it, I never went around to see Matsumoto to get a loan from him. We'd always sort things out on the phone, or else he'd bring the money to me. We couldn't have done things this way if we didn't trust each other completely.

Sadly, Matsumoto died in late 1985. His excellent wife—who would always greet me with a big smile and say, "Feel free to borrow as much as you'd like" when I applied for a loan from her husband—remains hale and hearty; and his two daughters are happily married.

Matsumoto's wife was a tremendous help to him. A bad wife means a lifetime of misery for a man. By the same token, what does a bad husband mean for a woman? That's a question I should probably ask my wives in the other world.

A Life
of Inspiration

People often describe me as a man of inspiration and impulse. I give this impression because of all my fantastic notions and crazy ideas, but I mean everything I say. I always want to put my ideas into practice as fast as I possibly can—that's the way I've always been. I'm impetuous, impulsive, a real hothead. Switching from one trade to another, devising pretexts for getting loans, cooking up pretty speeches to seduce women—all resulted from inspiration and improvisation. Persuading people with well-thought-out, logical arguments was never my forte.

I suspect this part of my character has a lot to do with how my brain is structured. Someone with a passion for knowledge can use his education as a tool of persuasion, but for someone like me who always detested schoolwork that was never a realistic option. I almost never read books. Almost none of what I had been taught at school penetrated my thick skull. As a result, the only thing I ever had to work with was the practical philosophy I had learned out in the real world. For me, the secret to making my way in the world was to exploit my sense of how people would react and to turn my grasp of human behavior into a weapon.

Of course, this sort of inspiration and intuition can be a double-edged sword. Sure, you can claim that you are mentally flexible and have an animal instinct for what will fly, but sometimes all that impulsive, off-the-cuff action can just be so much self-satisfied posturing. In my case, I was prone to charge headlong into things without worrying too much about the outcome—so it's hardly surprising that I failed so often! It never occurred to me that doing things in too much of a hurry could result in my making mistakes. I always believed that attack was the best form of defense.

When it comes to action, people can be divided into three broad types. One type is very cautious, never rushes into anything, and only makes a move after due and proper thought. Realists—people who think about what they're doing while they're doing it—constitute the second group. The third type charge into action too hastily and end up later having to sort out the mess they've created. This classification is a bit crude, but it's an interesting framework for analyzing and understanding character. The fact that each of the three groups can justify their way of doing things to themselves shows you how diverse people are—and how wily.

Which of the three groups do I belong to? The last one, of course. Once I get an idea, I'm not comfortable until I've acted on it. True to my zodiac, I'm a reckless, charging, wild boar kind of man. Rushing ahead without looking right or left has often left me with honorable—or maybe not so honorable—scars on my shins and shoulders. Then again, this lack of concern for myself may also account for my having survived for so long.

I have spent my whole life obsessed with business and reckon that I'm about twice as greedy as the average person. But my greed never went as far as avarice. I always took care to share any profits, and I am sure this is why my business partners and counterparts trusted me and ended up my friends. Trust is the natural outcome of refusing to hog profits and practicing share and share alike. In addition, it helps to have a "do-no-harm" attitude.

✧ ✧ ✧

In the mid-1930s, I was living in Awaza in Osaka and working as a broker of textiles and cloth. My employees were all relatives, and they made me a lot of money. While I wanted to make money, I was also determined that my profit should never come at another's loss. If you want the people you do business with to make money, too, then you should be able to avoid trouble and unpleasantness.

"Even if you yourself go bankrupt, make sure that you never cause anyone else any trouble." This philosophy may sound too good to be true, but I believe that if you communicate integrity to the people you're dealing with, then you are nearly guaranteed to reach an agreement. I hammered this lesson into my staff.

Around this time I got my son Tsuneo, in his mid-teens, to come to Osaka to help me. He had that special Shimane toughness and could put up with anything. While he was still just a boy, I had sent him out to hawk things like *konnyaku* (konjac, used in Japanese cooking) and the pictures people hang out at the Tanabata Festival. While he was in elementary school, I would always tell him that mastering business was much more important than going to school. I was probably far from a model parent, but I genuinely believed that getting a grip at an early age on how business worked would do him more good than a load of half-assed book-learning. A crummy education never helped anyone make money.

Tsuneo understood where I was coming from and buckled down. When you're running a small-scale business of your own, it's your own family—people you like and can trust under any circumstances—who make the best staff. Although he was still young, I sent Tsuneo out to call on all our regular customers like the rest of the staff.

❖ ❖ ❖

But times were hard. With the breakout of the Pacific War, the business environment became more and more difficult. Eventually in 1943 I had to restructure the firm and go back to my hometown. Mr. Shinoda and Matsumoto Yasutaro, a friend from the textile wholesaling business, joined me, in part because of safety concerns. Whenever I started a new venture, I usually looked to my tight circle of friends, and I was close to Shinoda and Matsumoto in business and in life.

Back in Yasugi, I had not yet thought in any detail about

what my next project would be. At a bar, I got into a conversation with an engineer from the local steel research labs of Hitachi. The two of us hit it off, and the discussion soon turned to the question of how to make money.

"I know we're in the middle of a war here, but isn't there something I could get into that would be of use to Japan?" I asked him.

"You could try pro-ducing swords for the

My oldest son, Tsuneo, and I, when he was in grade school; I was teaching him about business.

army and navy," he replied encouragingly. Before the war, Yasugi had been famous for two things: *dojosukui*, the local rustic dance, and its Hitachi metalworks. Looking over at Shinoda and Matsumoto who were in the bar with me, I asked them to come into business with me.

So we three, together with the Hitachi engineer, established the Izumo Sword Company in Hirose, with me as managing director, and the Tama Hagane Ironworks in Sekishu, with Matsumoto in charge. There were all sorts of shortages at the time, but we obviously needed a supply of iron and steel to make our swords. Sekishu had a long flourishing tradition of iron and steel manufacture using iron sands and the traditional clay-furnace *tatara* technique, as well as copper mining and smelting. The company had six or seven employees, including the female clerks. Children were then being mobilized for the war effort, so lots of girls from Hirose Elementary School helped. Children were either dispatched to farms or the factories in Yasugi and Amagasaki. The country's entire population was mobilized for the war effort.

When the time came for us to deliver our first batch of swords, a group of army captains and lieutenants in their forbidding uniforms came over from Koshibara in Matsue. They erected a straw dummy in the factory and started swinging away at it by way of product testing.

Every morning, I used to don a blue suit, stand in front of all the staff, and make a speech about how this was a time of crisis, the very survival of our country was at stake, and we all had to pull together. We used to sing the company song with great fervor.

Our company, our skills, our factory,
Crafting Japanese swords,
Swords that vanquish all danger.
For that day, that day of victory
Cheerfully, let us fight, comrades
Let us fight on together.

The song had a lofty fighting spirit. I had completely forgotten the lyrics, but Tanaka Chieko, the office manager at Nichibi in Osaka until last year, has a first-class memory and was able to jog mine. By a funny coincidence, she was one of the schoolgirls sent to the factory to help us so many years ago! It's strange to think that it wasn't only grown-ups who sang these martial songs, but girls and boys too. It was a harsh and brutal time.

Nonetheless, when it comes to business there's no holding me back. We acquired any raw materials we needed on the black market, and if we got an order for ten swords, we would make fifteen or sixteen and sell the extras on the side for a nice, fat profit. In an age when modern weapons like howitzers and rifles decided the outcome of wars, our carefully crafted traditional swords hardly represented the road to victory. The war went from bad to worse. I could not discuss it openly, but secretly I was thinking intently about what business I should move into at the war's end.

Convinced that Japan was doomed to defeat, I bought 420 acres of forested land nearby for 80,000 yen. Building materials were sure to be in demand to rebuild Japan's cities, which were being burned to the ground in air raids. I had this insight before anyone else and invested ahead of the pack. Since trees take forty or fifty years to grow to maturity, I had grand dreams of making money sometime in the future, even if things didn't work out in the short term.

Sure enough, timberland started rocketing in price soon after and I was offered 500,000 yen by someone keen to buy my holding. I was tempted, but my father persuaded me to sit tight and not sell.

Deciding to up the ante, I teamed up with Mr. Shinoda to acquire another 690 acres of forest in Sekishu for 240,000 yen. As I surveyed the outline of the green-clad mountains, I felt pleasantly sure that my capital was going to snowball. As far as I was concerned, there really was "gold in them thar' hills"!

Unfortunately, this scheme ended up going catastrophically wrong when people started importing foreign lumber, which was far cheaper than the Japanese product, in large quantities. It was a bitter disappointment when my money trees were suddenly transformed into so many useless sticks.

My frustration was all the more acute because of some advice that Kohara Yaichiro, a friend of mine in the wholesale textile business in Osaka, had given me just before I acquired my land. "Make your move right now," he told me, "and you can pick up 1 *tsubo* of land in the Senba district of downtown Osaka for the price of a single tatami mat.* It's a once-in-a-

---

* Land areas in Japan are often given in units of *tsubo*. 1 *tsubo* = approx. 36 square feet. 1 *tsubo* is twice the size of 1 tatami.

lifetime opportunity. Much better to buy land in town than out in the country."

It is hard to believe how cheap land was in those days, especially now when the frenzied rise of prices is a serious problem in Tokyo and other cities. Had I taken Kohara's advice, I would be enormously rich today. Kohara followed his own prescription. Hastily selling off the entire stock of garments he had stashed away when he left Osaka, he used the entire proceeds to buy up land in Senba—and is now, consequently, a very rich man. This episode gave me an acute sense of my inability to look around corners and see what the future holds!

In May 1945, my third son, Mikio, was born. After the war ended later that year, we reorganized the Izumo Sword Company and changed its name to Yamato Tool Works. No one was going to need swords anymore. After Japan's defeat, life was hard both in the cities and the country. No one had enough money to get by.

❖ ❖ ❖

On December 31, 1945, Shinoda, who had returned to Osaka before the rest of us, dropped in to our old family house in Furukawa to see me.

"The whole of Osaka has been burnt to the ground. There are shortages of everything—complete and total chaos. The police are nowhere to be seen, and the black market is in full swing," he explained. "So, all-in-all it looks to me like an unbeatable opportunity to coin it. Get together about 500,000 yen and come over and join me. I've no money of my own, but my house in the city is still standing. You're welcome to stay with me, so let's get a move on and go into business."

Knowing my knack for raising loans, Shinoda asked me to raise the necessary seed money before going down to Osaka. Needless to say, I didn't feel like staying in Yasugi forever and was secretly aching to move back to the big city. Shinoda and I felt the same—we wanted to get back to doing business in our old stomping grounds in Osaka as soon as possible.

I quickly decided to approach a man who had been running a steelworks in Osaka and had come back to Yasugi after getting 4 million yen for military procurements. He was a pretty funny guy. Occasionally he would sing out, "Please, please, please, take care of me," while making the gesture for "woman" by sticking his pinky finger out of his clenched fist. As I had introduced him to quite a number of ladies, we had something of a bond. When he had gotten hold of a truckload of cotton cloth sold cheaply by the army, he was nice enough to let me have it at a knockdown price. I had made 150,000 yen from the sale, so I only needed to raise another 350,000.

It is considered unlucky to get into debt too early in a new year, so I waited until a few days after the weeklong holiday to approach him about the money. He agreed without a moment's hesitation.

"I'll leave the interest rate up to you," he said. The conditions were even better than I could have hoped. Again I saw how important it was to be trusted.

Having raised the money, I set off by myself for Osaka on January 11, 1946. I stayed with Shinoda at his house in Fukushima for some time, and together we went into the textile business with 500,000 yen in capital.

Things went fantastically. We were clearing 10,000 yen a day, and our profits increased to 1 million in no time. After repaying the original capital, we split the remaining 500,000 yen, and I decided to go back to Yasugi. I always wanted to double my capital before returning to my hometown. That was my rule of thumb, and I was very single-minded about it. I don't mean to boast, but I never returned home broke.

My appetite for money and my interest in women are both about twice that of the average man. Follow my career and

A photograph from around the time I started up the Izumo Sword Company.

you are guaranteed to find women flitting in and out of the picture. I fear this is a sickness that only death will cure!

The day I left Osaka for Yasugi, I exchanged my old yen for new yen, and crammed 750,000 yen's worth of 100-yen notes into a trunk. The bundle of notes was so huge that the bank teller had been very nervous. "It's dangerous to walk around with so much money," he said. "We'll get you a guard."

I boarded the train in Osaka, but I was forced to cool my heels in Kyoto since the San'in Line terminated there. It was still cold, and there was no way I was going to spend the night outside. I tried to get a bed at one of the inns near the station, but even if they had empty rooms none of them wanted to accommodate a single person. In those disorderly times, nobody wanted to rent a room to someone who was traveling alone and about whom they knew nothing.

As I was leaving the umpteenth inn to reject me, an elegant middle-aged woman in a Japanese kimono passed me on her way in. I could tell from her face that she too was looking for somewhere to spend the night. I guessed that she was probably also being turned down by everyone, and I waited for her outside. Sure enough, out she came looking thoroughly dejected. It was just what I wanted.

"It looks to me as though your request for a room was

turned down. The truth is, I'm traveling alone too. Like you, lots of inns have turned me away and I'm getting a bit tired of it. I really don't want to spend the night out in the open. Would you be willing to pose as my companion and share a room with me?" I proposed.

"Yes, I would," she said. She must have been having a very hard time to agree so readily.

We managed to secure a room and I pressed a tip into the maid's hands, telling her I wanted her to get me some black-market sake and that I didn't care about the price. My lady companion turned out to be quite a drinker and had a delicious, sultry voice. I was in a great mood as we poured each other drinks and chatted about all sorts of things.

She told me that she lived in Tottori with her husband who was sixty and worked in the law courts. She was his second wife and taught the *koto*. Her manners and her dress showed her to be a married woman of a certain social standing. She was beautiful—petite and a little plump, exactly my type—and had oodles of sex appeal.

Naturally enough, I wanted to make a good impression. Although I was running a tiny textile wholesaler in Fukushima all by myself, I pretended that I was the manager of a decent-sized firm in Senba and even gave her an invented phone number for it. I did my best to come across as a proper little captain of industry.

We both began to get a little tipsy. The maid told us the bath was ready, so we took turns keeping an eye on the luggage while the other went off for a soak. The maid meanwhile spread out the bedding—one futon with two pillows. The woman became rather flustered when she saw this.

"Don't worry," I said in an effort to reassure her. "I won't do anything." But I was a man and she a woman, and once we were in bed together the inevitable happened.

The next morning, I remembered that I needed to make

a few calls. "There's something valuable in my trunk there," I impressed upon her before leaving the room. "Make sure to stay in the room until I get back."

In those days, hotel rooms did not have their own phones. You had to make your way to wherever the one phone was to make your call. That took a while, and then all calls had to be routed through the operator. It was quite a hassle.

After she had been waiting quite some time, the woman suddenly had to hurry off to the toilet. In the few minutes that she was out of the room, my trunk was fine—but her alligator skin handbag was stolen! It had contained almost 3,000 yen, she told me.

The poor woman was crushed and turned white as a sheet. Our dreamy romance of a few moments ago had turned into a nightmare of remorse that was eating her up. Since I was partly responsible for what had happened, I could not ignore her plight, but when I handed her 5,000 yen, she looked, to use the Japanese expression, as if she had bumped into Buddha in the middle of hell.

"I promise I'll pay you back. Oh, I don't know how to thank you. But thank you, thank you so much," she said as she left, bowing low and often. She went back to Tottori on the first morning train. I never saw her again.

She was my kind of woman. And to think even now she could be calling the wrong phone number I gave her, I feel a tug on my heartstrings. How much I regretted not having told her my real number! Of the women in my life, she was definitely one of the top two. My remembering her so well after so long gives you an idea of just how chagrined I am. I was always quick to make my move on a woman, but at crucial times I messed up.

I am the first to admit that I have a tendency to fool around, but I have never initiated a break-up. Either we agreed to part, death intervened, or a woman left me under her own steam. I take comfort knowing that my relationships ended without any hard feelings.

My experience in Kyoto made me see that when you tell lies you often end up hurting yourself. Tell even a single lie, and you can never take it back. Sometimes it will torment you for ages, forcing you to tell ten times as many lies to cover up that first one. The only time it's okay to lie is when you're having a fling behind your wife's back.

As you can see from this episode, when I wasn't wheeling and dealing I was chasing skirts, so what with one thing or another, I was rushed off my feet. Back in Yasugi, I was under pressure to clear the backlog of work left by the sword and steel companies.

Tsuneo, my eldest son, who had been in Yasugi since being evacuated from Osaka, got married in October 1946. He was twenty-three. We often used to go down to the Shuku River together during the cherry-blossom season. Because of all the boozing that takes place, I've always found that fistfights go with cherry blossoms, the way *daikon* radishes go so well with mackerel. Straightforward and frank to a fault, I always managed to cause trouble. I believed in striking first and talking later. If someone was looking for a fight, I was not going to turn them down—that's the kind of fellow I am.

My tactics were to deliver a flurry of punches the instant my opponent and I had squared off, then bolt like a rabbit. My son had a more easygoing approach to fighting. As a result, he often ended up getting caught and quite badly pummeled. "I'm never going cherry-blossom viewing with you again, Dad," he would grumble. What a despicable and selfish father I was to run off and leave my son alone like that! I'm so sorry, so very sorry.

✣ ✣ ✣

In 1947, the ownership of Yamato Tools Works was transferred, enabling me to leave my hometown and settle down properly in Osaka. I started a new life, biking around the burnt-out ruins of Osaka every day. I was trying to make a living among the traders of Osaka who were, as the Japanese saying goes, "wily enough to steal the eyes out of a living horse." To succeed against them, you had to be totally committed. I had to work not three, but five, maybe even ten times as hard as a normal man.

In January 1949, I set up Maruzen Textiles, a cloth wholesaler, in Karamonomachi in Senba. This company would later become one of the pillars of my commercial success. More than thirty years had passed since my first business venture with my handcart and my first stint in Osaka immediately after leaving the army. In the interim, I had owned shops in Fukushima and Awaza, but my life had been emotionally rootless. Owning a shop in Senba—the mecca of wholesaling and finance in Osaka—boosted my business significantly and earned me, I felt, a greater degree of trust. This marked the turning point for me as a businessman.

Struggles
in Senba

As a child, I hated studying, but art was the one subject I liked. As an adult, I was so engrossed in my business that for years I didn't have the time to turn my attention to art or anything like that. Moneymaking was my only interest. Some people say that a degree of inner tranquillity is the secret to business success, but I think that it all comes down to character. I am a volatile person, and my best ideas often come to me when I'm under pressure. "When the going gets tough, the tough get going," as they say. I had not lost my childhood fondness for art. It had just been forced into hibernation because I was so busy.

I had not thought about art in several years, when one day—it must have been 1947 or '48—I was cycling along Shinsaibashi Boulevard in Osaka. A couple of hanging scrolls in the window of a run-down antique shop caught my eye; one showed the rising sun, the other Mount Fuji. The rising sun picture made such a powerful impression on me that I dismounted to get a better look. The artist was named Yokoyama Taikan, and the painting was *Mount Penglai (Mountain of Immortals)*. This was the first time I had encountered Yokoyama Taikan's work. The painting, I remember, cost 80,000 yen and was about 30 inches high.

In those days, 1 *tsubo* of Senba real estate went for 3,000 yen, so this single painting cost as much as 26 *tsubo* of land. The price was way beyond my grasp, but the more I looked at the picture, the more I wanted it, so I made a point of cycling past the shop whenever I found myself with time to kill.

Mount Penglai is a holy mountain. According to the old Chinese chronicles, "A hermit lives on the magic mountain of Penglai. He possesses an elixir that will stop you from growing old and save you from death. . . ." When I looked at the magnificent picture, it gave me a cool and soothing sensation of calm, which was a new feeling for me. I was experiencing the magical power of art. I ought to mention that the other picture, the one of Mount Fuji, was the work of Hashimoto Kansetsu and cost 80,000 yen, too. I liked the Hashimoto, but had I been told to choose, I would definitely have decided in favor of the Taikan.

I sat down on the pavement, folded my arms, and reviewed my options. Was there any way I could buy the thing? No. No matter how I thought about it, it was impossible—plain and simple. Very much against my will, I had to give up. Human nature being what it is, of course, this setback only made me want it more. The prey that escapes the hunter is the one he wants to catch the most. As I gazed at the painting I promised myself that one day, come hell or high water, I *would* buy myself a Yokoyama Taikan. This was the origin of my bond with Taikan.

I acquired a book of his paintings not long afterward. It was the catalog of the 1940 *Ten Scenes of the Sea and Ten Scenes of Mount Fuji* exhibition that had been held to mark the 2,600th anniversary of the Imperial Era. The exhibition was a monumental retrospective in which Taikan had shown work from his fifty-year career. All the works were pervaded with the grand spirit of an artist who genuinely loved his country. Taikan himself said: "I want people to look at the emotion in my paintings, not at their technical proficiency. My goal is to express through art the spirit common to all Japanese."

The twenty works of Mount Fuji and the sea were sold for 25,000 yen apiece—an extraordinary price when you think that a good Taikan in those days usually went for only about 3,000 yen. Nonetheless the paintings sold out in record time. Taikan donated the entire 500,000-yen proceeds to the Ministry of War. The public was very taken with the idea that the money would be used to build a fighter plane called the *Taikan*. This plan was typical of Yokoyama Taikan, who was a fervent patriot. This 1940 exhibition boosted both his celebrity and the value of his paintings.

This group of twenty works became something of an

obsession for me. All I had to go on was the catalog, but it was enough to give me a vivid impression of Taikan's ideas and extraordinary powers of expression. When I first saw *Mountain after a Shower* in the *Ten Scenes of Mount Fuji* series, it moved me so profoundly that I started trembling all over. I liked it so much that I cut the reproduction out of the book, framed it, and kept it hanging in my room for well over a decade. I have never done anything like that with a reproduction before or since, but this particular picture, I felt, had revealed the force of a true masterpiece to me.

I was destined to encounter the real *Mountain after a Shower* under dramatic circumstances some thirty or so years later, an episode I will describe fully at the proper time. My encounters with works of art are no less important than my encounters with people, and both are like flowers that bloom along this road we call life.

My connection to Taikan gradually grew deeper. The first of his paintings I acquired was *Cuckoo*, a hanging scroll about 2 feet high, and registered as No. 1 in the catalog of my Taikan collection. I must have bought it in either 1957 or 1958. If I remember right, it cost me 250,000 yen. A peaceful and delicate work, it shows a cuckoo gliding above a lake. I was very fond of the picture, but ended up having to sell it. Later I hunted for it high and low, but we were not to meet again. Maybe that was destiny. . . .

✤ ✤ ✤

As I grew more interested in art, I also started to feel more enthusiastic about business. I had a source of emotional fulfillment that energized me. In January 1949, I established Maruzen Textiles, a cotton cloth wholesaler, at 3-20 Karamonomachi in Osaka with myself as managing director. The shop occupied about 30 *tsubo* on a corner of a street with all the Dobuike wholesalers. (I am currently renting out the Maruzen building to a clothing shop.) The Maruzen logo—a circle (*maru* in Japanese) containing the character *zen*—is painted on the upstairs facade of the corner of the building that overlooks the intersection. Seeing the gold still shining away undimmed after all these years makes me feel nostalgic.

Textiles was my main business, but I also had interests in money lending and selling imported cars. Since I was so busy, I got Tsuneo, my eldest son, who had recently married, to come down from Yasugi with his family to help me out. My wife and I lived above the shop in Senba, while Tsuneo and his family lived in Imazato in Higashinari.

Two or three years before, I had hired a man I shall call "Mr. A." Since he had a pretty good sense of business and was a good talker, competent, and quick on his feet, I was happy to delegate all my important tasks to him. When I became chairman, I planned to appoint him CEO. Just as I had expected, he worked hard and did a good job. He was a self-starter who personally visited our clients to help increase sales. But he would soon stab me in the back.

I am not the kind of person who likes being in business on my own. I don't feel comfortable unless I'm working with a partner or high-quality staff. As I didn't have the foggiest notion about accounting, I had to get someone to take care of that side of things for me. I had a perfectly good head for numbers, but bookkeeping was never my forte. Perhaps memories of being the school dunce lingered in the back of my mind, but my doubts about my own abilities made me very willing to trust other people, and once I decided to trust someone, I trusted them implicitly. As a result, I often ended up being cheated and betrayed.

"Good-natured and innocent" would be a nice way to describe me, but I was frankly a bit of an idiot. Obviously, the person who cheats is worse than the person who gets cheated, but you can't deny that the victims, by laying themselves open to being tricked, bear some responsibility. I'm a good example, and this is not just sour grapes at being outsmarted. It's better to be cheated by someone than to cheat someone else because you don't suffer any pangs of conscience.

Textiles was the right business to be in at that time; my company was performing fantastically. For some years after the war, the textile business was the main engine of the Japanese economy, and Senba was really heaving. It was a chaotic, anything-goes era—and a great time to make money. As my capital grew, I started buying pieces of real estate here and there and gradually expanded into the property business.

❖ ❖ ❖

In May 1951, I bought Amagasaki Automobile Industries, a foreign car importer, and appointed myself chairman and managing director. At the time Japanese people were restricted from owning foreign cars. As a result, our clients were either soldiers in the Occupation army or buyers from overseas. Since you could only import a handful of cars at a time, you were guaranteed buyers the instant a shipment came in, so it seemed like a good business.

After we had sold a certain number of cars, however, demand fell off a cliff. We had quite simply run out of buyers! To keep the business going, we had to get letters of credit (a kind of payment guarantee) from the bank every time we accepted a new delivery. The business had reached a dead end. We could only hope that a law would soon be passed permitting Japanese citizens to own foreign cars. But we never got wind that any such change was in the offing, and when we tried to get information from the Americans, the fact that none of us could speak English was a major stumbling block!

At that point a former member of parliament who was

Happy in our comfortable Bishoen home with my wife, Masako.

running a bus and taxi company in Tokyo suggested that I sell him the firm right away. My colleague Mr. A was strongly in favor of the deal.

"You can't afford to bleed any more red ink," he argued. "It's destroying your reputation. The sooner you sell the firm and get rid of it the better."

I had a hunch that I'd be better off sitting tight a little longer, but with everyone making such a hoo-ha, I reluctantly sold the firm, which was only a year old, for next to nothing to the former MP in May of the following year.

Just three months after the sale went through, the law was revised so that Japanese people could own foreign cars. A model that previously would not have moved off the lot below cost at 150,000 yen was now in such demand that it sold for a premium at 800,000 yen. You can imagine my vexation. If I had only hung in there a little longer, I could have been making money hand over fist. Since the company also came with 1,500 *tsubo* of land right next to a national road, I also missed out on the chance to make more than 100 million yen from real estate. I berated myself for being too naive to see people's real motives.

I owned another company called Heiwa Sangyo on

Dobuike New Road. Heiwa was the owner of a two-story building that was rented out to around twenty tenants in the textile
business. It was an enormously profitable property. The tenants' deposits more than covered the cost of the land and the
building, so whatever they paid in rent was pure profit.

And then I was told: "Everybody's saying that Maruzen
isn't committed to its main textile business anymore since it
became so interested in real estate. What should I tell people
who say that? It's getting so hard to do my job. If Maruzen Textiles means anything to you, you should sell that building off
right away." When the matter was presented to me persuasively
like this, I ended up selling the building off cheaply to one of
the tenants.

✤ ✤ ✤

In September 1962, the year after I sold Amagasaki Automobile
Industries, I set up Shin-Osaka Tochi, a real estate company, in
Higobashi in Nishi-ku. Daido Life Insurance and I put up the
capital. I had talked over my plans with Masumura Takeshi,
Daido's Chairman and CEO. He trusted me and agreed to
work with me. He has been unstintingly generous to me with
his expert advice on accounting and moneymaking opportunities ever since.

Ms. Hattori Ritsu, one of my office clerks (now CEO of
Nichibi), was a big help in setting up Shin-Osaka Tochi. I had
met her father, who had been in charge of the mill for Sumi-
nokura Cotton, through work. I arranged for her to join the
company as soon as she graduated from school. She was such
an efficient worker that Masumura Takeshi couldn't praise her
enough. "I've worked with plenty of female clerks in my time,"
he said, "but I've never seen one who showed so much initiative
or worked so hard right after joining the firm."

Her extraordinary abilities caught my attention. Clearly,

it would have been a waste to leave her with the very limited responsibilities most women had at the time. She always gave me moral support when I got depressed by all the problems Maruzen Textiles, my other company, was suffering.

Mr. A., who knew I was a sucker for flattery, used to butter me up: "The president of a company like you should be living in a house more worthy of his status. I hear that an excellent property is on the market in Bishoen. Why don't you move?"

I followed his advice and left the second-floor flat above the company premises in Senba for a grand mansion in Bishoen. It was only when I was forced to sell the house several years later that I learned it was registered in the company's name and not mine. By contrast, when Mr. A. bought himself a house, he made certain to put it in his own name despite borrowing the money he needed to buy it from the company.

Trying his luck speculating in the cotton markets, it was not long before Mr. A. had dug the firm into a deep financial hole. Without the slightest trace of guilt, he eventually told me that he would accept responsibility for the trouble he had caused the company and resign forthwith.

"What are you talking about?" I countered. "The running of the entire company was in your hands so you're responsible for the losses. You can't just get up and leave! If you'd said you were going to make good the loss and *then* leave, that would be different, but this is the height of irresponsibility!" Despite my attempts to change his mind, Mr. A. left and set up on his own.

He went to visit all our best suppliers. "This new company we're just starting up now is our *real* company," he told them. "We don't want you to sell to Maruzen anymore. Mr. Adachi has agreed to be chairman of the new firm." Unsurprisingly, that bit about making me chairman was an empty promise.

I worked like crazy trying to fill the hole that Mr. A. had opened up in the company balance sheet. My first step was to change my own lifestyle. I sold the mansion I had moved into less than two years earlier to Otani Takejiro, one of the founders of the Shochiku movie studio. Otani was not interested in taking the living room furniture along with the house, so I approached my friend Kohara Yaichiro, who was in the same business as me in Senba, about buying it. "There's a more pressing issue to deal with here," Kohara replied, abruptly changing the subject. "What are you going to do about a place to live?"

"My wife and I discussed it, and we're planning to rent an apartment and start over."

"Listen, I have a house over in Senba. It's 150 *tsubo* and it's unoccupied. At some point I'm going to sell it, but that won't be for a while. I'd be happy if you moved in there. It's better than leaving the place empty. I wouldn't normally do this, but you, you're special."

"Well, I'll take you at your word, then. How much is the rent?"

"Rent! What are you talking about? I wouldn't be lending you the place if I planned to charge for it. I don't need any rent. My only condition is you'll up and leave when I decide to sell the house."

As soon as I got home, I talked it over with my wife. "I think it would be better for us to find a cheap apartment and pay proper rent than be lent a place for nothing," she argued. "That would be less awkward for you, wouldn't it?"

Trust the wife, I thought admiringly. But hang on a minute.

"Nothing costs you more than something that's free" goes the old saying, but nobody's going to say that they're happy to give you something for nothing, unless they trust you. Rather than look a gift horse in the mouth, I felt I should accept the offer in the same kind spirit in which it had been made, and make an appropriate expression of my gratitude later when I could. I managed to convince my wife and took up Kohara on his good-natured offer. Trust is indeed the highest expression of friendship.

While we were living in this loaned accommodation, I suffered so much from stress that I had stomach and liver problems. Word of this reached Mr. A. who came to visit.

"I know a good hospital in Tokyo," he said, as brazen as ever. "Let me take you there. Anything you need—anything at all—just let me know."

I was a physical and mental wreck. I thought that for once maybe even he would understand.

"Look, you can see the state I'm in. I couldn't go anywhere, even if I wanted to. Can't you look after both our companies, yours and mine?" I asked him. I was clutching at straws.

"No need to play the shrinking violet. Just leave it to me. I'll take care of everything," he said, and wrung my hand. "You just concentrate on getting better as fast as you can. I owe you so much. Everything I have, I owe to you."

His reaction was hugely comforting to me, sick and bedridden as I was. Mistakenly thinking that a friend in need was a friend indeed, I trusted him. I was surprised when he showed no sign of leaving.

"You'd better get busy," I coaxed. "There's a lot of business that needs doing."

"Don't worry, I've got a few things cooking right now," he said. "You've got a couple of salesmen in your firm. Now, could you see your way to firing them?"

I asked him why.

"Look into the accounts, and you'll see you simply don't have the resources to pay out high salaries."

"That's true, but if they go, then there'll be no one selling for us," I objected. "That'll kill the business."

Mr. A. insisted that he would take care of things himself, so I set up the salesmen independently, letting them take their clients with them. I expected that Mr. A. would now start doing his job, but he continued doing nothing. I pressed him for an explanation.

"I've tried my best," he said, "but it's no good. I'll need your help winding things up."

I fairly blew my top. If the fellow had been planning to run my company into the ground, then he really didn't need to go through the charade of consulting me in the first place.

"Enough!" I yelled, thumping the desk. "Do you think I'm a complete idiot!"

❖ ❖ ❖

My wife and I spent three years living in the house Kohara lent us. In 1956 we bought a house in a little lane in Uehonmachi 6 where we lived together with my son's family, who had previously been living in Higashinari Ward. My son and his wife had two children, so for the first time since moving to Osaka we were living in a normal three-generation family. Incidentally, my grandson, Adachi Takanori, is now the director of the Adachi Museum of Art, while my granddaughter, Okubo Tokiko, is a qualified curator deeply involved with the museum, too.

The house in Uehonmachi was a two-story, U-shaped building. We built a new entrance in a corner of the upper floor and divided it up into apartments so we could rent the space to a couple of families. We were forced to turn our own house into a supplementary source of income because of the financial damage I had suffered at the hands of Mr. A. But I didn't care what people said about me.

Life was so difficult that I had trouble getting to sleep at night. One night, after I drank a whole bottle of whiskey, I ended up sleeping for three days and three nights straight, groaning all the while. At one point, I thought that doing some singing might help cheer me up, so I went out and bought a record of Minami Haruo's "Hello, Sailor." I practiced singing along with it, but when I realized how tone-deaf I was I felt even more miserable.

After I had sold my own mansion in Bishoen, I tried desperately to persuade Mr. A. to sell his house so he could pay off the company's debts. He always snuck off after saying he'd get right on it or something like that. Of course, he never paid a penny in the end.

During this period the local bank, without a word of warning, suddenly took possession of the 440 acres of forest that I owned in Nunobe, Hirose, near my hometown. Repossession notices were posted at the bottom of the three roads that led up the mountainside. One reason for the bank's action was that I was three months behind on the payments. When I checked up on things, however, it turned out that Mr. A. had been busily spreading the rumor that Maruzen Textiles was in serious trouble. Taking his lies at face value, the bank had acted without bothering to make any inquiries of the people directly involved, i.e., me. We had a long-standing business relationship, so I charged into the bank and made a big scene. The director overseeing my accounts sent a message that he was out and cowered somewhere in a back office.

"Come on out and show your face!" I yelled. "You may be lending me money, but this is outrageous."

I scraped together the money I owed by the due date. Then I told them I would never do business with them again and walked out of the bank, bringing our relationship to an abrupt end.

In my hometown, a number of local people had bought shares in Shin-Osaka Tochi, the real estate company I had founded with Daido Life Insurance. After we had been unable to make any dividend payments for a while, these locals wanted to sell their shares and hoped I would buy them.

I was in trouble because the sums involved were massive. I went to get advice from Masumura Takeshi, who introduced me to Okahashi Seizaimon, a famous "forestry king" and the scion of a rich family in Nara Prefecture. Sure enough, Okahashi was a man of great dignity and poise. He was good-hearted and understood the position I was in, so our discussions proceeded rapidly.

"I'll take all those shares off your hands," he said.

This was a better response than I could have hoped for. Okahashi's father had been the president of the Nanto Bank and an important man, but Okahashi himself was also far from average. Thanks to him, I was able to pay the shareholders a premium on the face value of the shares.

Okahashi presented me with the stone lantern that stands in the Adachi Museum's White Gravel and Pine Garden, and also pressed Tomioka Tessai's *Mount Penglai* into my hands. He is one of my great benefactors and helped make me what I am today.

I could not reveal Mr. A.'s treachery to anyone else. Worried that my most valuable colleagues would be horrified and shun me if they knew what was going on, I had to suffer in silence. Some years after the museum had opened, Mr. A. invited me to the wedding of his eldest son. "I want you to come," he said. "I'm reserving the seat of honor for you."

With age I have become more tolerant, but Mr. A. is the one person I can never forgive. In the ten years after meeting him, my life turned into a frantic exercise in damage control. There was nothing positive about it—it was the toughest time of my life.

During these difficult years in around 1958 or '59, I teamed up with Matsumoto Shigeru and Hattori Ritsu to establish a firm called Heiwa Sightseeing. I may have been wounded, but the fighting spirit hadn't been knocked out of me. We built the Food Center Building in Umeda, one of the busiest districts in central Osaka. The plan was to rent out all four floors for bars and restaurants.

That, at least, was our intention. Thanks in part to the excellent location, things went well at the beginning, but over time the building had some structural problems and we ended up having to sell it after a few years. During this period, Hattori worked incredibly hard for very little pay. With cafes and tea shops on every floor, the building proved a great commercial success. This is a classic example of how a small change in approach to a problem is all that separates success and failure.

On reflection, I can see that I generally had good basic concepts but failed to pay proper attention to all sorts of other things. With this building, my lack of patience and hasty execution were my undoing.

✦ ✦ ✦

Money lending was another business I tried during this time. The area between ultra-high-interest loans and ordinary bank loans looked promising to me, and I was something of a pioneer in the field. One of my major clients was a gynecological hospital in Minami in Osaka. On the surface it looked like a very august institution, but financially it was a basket case. I went to see the director in his office and found an older man with stubble on his chin. Wearing a white coat, he was slumped over his desk.

"We were having trouble balancing the books, so we stupidly went and borrowed money from some gangsters," he wailed. "Now they're harassing me and I'm at the end of my rope. It would be a lifesaver if you could give us an injection of capital."

My heart went out to the hospital director who was clearly under a great strain. I lent him 40 million yen. I always had a keen sense of justice and could never desert a person in trouble.

The hospital made the first repayment on time; but when

the second one was due, nothing happened—complete silence. I hurried to see the director and find out what was going on. His attitude to me could not have been more different.

"There's nothing I can do about money we don't have," he insisted aggressively.

Realizing there was something funny afoot, I consulted a professional.

"The borrower has a reputation to uphold," I was told. "So if you tell him you're going to get a bankruptcy judgment against him, you can probably force him to pay you back."

I followed this advice.

"Go ahead and try," was the director's response.

Completely unfazed, he even dared to provoke me. Furious, I submitted a petition to the court for a declaration of bankruptcy. The hospital director seemed to have been expecting this and accepted the declaration without contesting it. His interpretation of the law was the opposite of mine: He thought that a bankrupt party had no obligation to pay back his debts. I tried to have the land and the hospital buildings placed under distraint, but was thwarted when they turned out to be in the director's brother's name. I was obviously dealing with a pair of veteran swindlers.

I then realized how frightening the world is; you can never say, "I've seen it all. This is rock bottom." It was also made painfully clear to me that I wasn't cut out for finance. I was a much better borrower than lender!

✢ ✢ ✢

I have one more awful, unforgettable experience connected to money. I had an acquaintance—let us call him Mr. C.—who owned a real estate company. He dropped by to see me one day because he needed money urgently. Taking his promissory note as security, I advanced him a loan.

The day he was due to repay the money came and went with no sign of him. When I took the promissory note to the bank, the bank refused to honor it because the space on the document for printing one's seal was ever so slightly in the wrong place. I had trusted the man implicitly—something that made his double-dealing all the more unforgivable. I asked a friend for advice on how to get my money back.

"That C. is a notorious villain. Ordinary methods won't stand a chance with him. Leave this to me," he advised me.

My friend sounded so sure of himself that I was confident everything would work out fine. A few days later, however, the police came charging into my place and announced they were arresting me for acts of violence. It was completely out the blue, and I was dumbfounded. Normally I would have given them an earful, but the police were so aggressive that I felt helplessly out of my depth. It took time before I could speak.

"Tell me what it is I'm supposed to have done wrong," I begged.

One of the policemen then read out a statement that said I had sent some gangsters around to C.'s to beat him up. I had no idea what they were talking about. Had my friend's idea of taking care of Mr. C. meant turning to the *yakuza* gangster mob? My jaw dropped. I was speechless.

I was locked up for a week in the cells in Osaka's Minato Police Station and then sent to the detention center. I ended up spending twenty days in detention all told. It was, I hasten to add, my first experience of life behind bars. I had no rights—nothing. They made me strip naked and noted my "distinctive physical marks," while completely ignoring my character. It was horrible. When they spoke to me, they used my surname without saying "mister."

The cell I was in had a wooden floor and was about the size of four-and-a-half tatami mats. I shared it with five very dodgy characters. The room was completely bare with a single toilet and nothing else. The toilet was surrounded by a glass partition, meaning everybody could see what you were doing. A person with normal sensitivities could never do his business in such conditions. I pleaded a stomachache while everyone else was out getting some sun and finally managed to do what I had to.

Life in the detention center was disgusting. The place was crawling with lice; the bath water was too filthy to get into; and the stench was vile. What dismayed me most were the people I was in there with—gangsters, thieves, swindlers, and violent criminals. My first few days inside they gave me a really hard time, but then everything suddenly changed.

"Mr. Adachi, you don't want to sit over in the corner like that," said the men, clustering around me. "Please come and sit in the middle of the room here."

"No, no. I'm just fine where I am."

"We can't allow that. We all want you to be nice and comfy, isn't that right?"

"Right. An important gent like yourself, Mr. Adachi, sitting in a cramped spot like that. It ain't right."

I figured out what happened. Before this point they'd all been yelling at me and calling me "Adachi," but they had somehow gotten wind of the fact that I was a company president. As a result, they had done a complete about-face and were now making a clumsy effort to be friendly and respectful. They were obviously hoping that I would return the favor when I got out. Or maybe they changed because I always shared the food parcels people sent me. Either way, once I had understood what was going on, I decided to accept their kindnesses. If things got desperate, I could just run away.

"Well, thank you. Don't mind if I do."

"Don't hold back, chief. Stretch your legs out. That's it. Lean back. Would you like a shoulder rub?"

"I don't think that'll be necessary."

"Really, sir, we've nothing better to do, we're bored in here and we're happy to do whatever you want. Hey, young fella," barked a grizzled old-timer to a scrawny small-time thief. "Get a move on and give Mr. Adachi here a shoulder massage."

I felt as though I had been magically transformed into the legendary 19th-century gangster Shimizu no Jirocho. Was there really so much prestige in being a company president? Until the day before, the atmosphere had been heavy with the threat of violence. I wouldn't have been surprised to get a good kicking. Now that all seemed like a bad dream.

"You should have told us you were the president of Maruzen, and we'd have treated you properly. You didn't say nothing about it. That's the only reason we gave you a hard time."

"You all know Maruzen, do you?"

"Are you teasing, boss? Course we know. We're not complete social rejects," said the old-timer. "Hey, Foxy, you knew about Maruzen, dincha?" He jerked his chin at a vile, sly-looking sixty-year-old with foxy eyes who had plopped down next him.

"Sure, I did. I mean, there's only one Maruzen Petroleum, right? Funny old world. Never expected to have the honor of meeting the boss of Maruzen in here of all places!"

I blinked in surprise. I couldn't stop myself. They had heard the name Maruzen and mistakenly assumed that my company, Maruzen Textiles, was Maruzen Petroleum. I hadn't lied to them, but there was no telling what they might do if I told them the truth. I decided to keep up the pretense. After all, it wouldn't be very nice of me to destroy their little fantasy.

Thanks to my cellmates, who were like characters from a comic book, I managed to put up with my long stretch in the detention center. I had fallen as low as I could go, but my presence there had sparked this farce of mistaken identity. I didn't know whether to laugh or cry. It's the story of my life!

One day the guard on duty called me out of the cell. I

went into the interview room and, who should be there, but Mr. C., the man responsible for the whole mess. The prosecutor had summoned him because he had found something suspicious about the discrepancies between my statement and his charges.

"If there's anything you want to get off your chest, Adachi, feel free to say it to this gentleman here," the prosecutor said. "I will just sit in and listen."

This was the signal for me to fly into a towering rage. Whenever I'd tried to say anything before, the prosecutor had always shut me up. "That's enough from you. All we need from you is a 'yes' or 'no' in reply to my questions." Now this arrogant man was giving me free rein. I've always had plenty to say for myself, but now all my pent-up emotion exploded in one mighty eruption.

"C., you bastard. You didn't just trick me out of my money, you went and got me locked up in this damn place, too. Have you got an ounce of compassion? You're a dirty little fraudster. It shouldn't be me, it should be *you* in here. You said you were in trouble, so I got the money together. I did you a favor, didn't I? If you were a normal human being—which you're not—you'd have come rushing over to explain the situation to the police and apologize to me. I can't believe how you can sit there looking as if you are innocent!"

I was so angry that my hands were shaking uncontrollably. I abused C. nonstop for about an hour while he just sat there in silence and listened. It wasn't enough for me. I was just about to start laying into him again, when the prosecutor, who had been there all along, declared, "Well, C., if what we heard just now was the truth, then even if I can't officially say you committed a fraud, it looks pretty borderline to me."

"Mr. Adachi, will you come with me?" He invited me into the room next door. He had never called me "mister" before.

"I think I have finally understood what happened. I believe

your account of things," he explained. "I am going to take care of the necessary paperwork so that you can get out of here immediately. I also recommend that you sue C. for fraud."

I didn't care about that. My only concern was to get out of that place as fast as I could.

"Thank you, but no. I just want to get out of here—and I never want to come back." I was so mentally and physically drained that tears were falling uncontrollably down my cheeks.

The prosecutor gave me a sympathetic smile. "All right, then. Collect your things discreetly so no one notices what you're up to. There's always a chance someone might follow you home. You must be careful. This isn't a place that respectable people frequent," he said and gave me another grin.

In the end, one gangster got a sentence for violence, while the case against me was dismissed. I later got to know the prosecutor quite well. He told me I should feel free to call him if a bunch of hired thugs ever came to visit me again. Sure enough, a small gang of them did appear at my place, but the instant I mentioned the prosecutor's name, they left and never came back.

In the end, I never filed charges. C. was a notorious villain without a shred of decency. It was painful to have to accept what had happened to me, but my priority was to cut all ties with scum like him. I didn't want to go to court, because all sorts of stuff—some true, some false—would have been said about me, and I would have been pilloried. My life was the same old, risky high-wire act. No sooner had I made some money here, than I ended up losing it all there. When was I going to find peace and stability?

During these years, I was groping my way forward, without really knowing what I was doing.

In Other
People I Trust

I t's often said that people only turn to God when things become difficult for them. In my case, when the going gets tough, it's not God I turn to, but other people. When C. had turned against me like a docile dog that suddenly savages its master, a number of kindhearted people came to my aid, people who tower as far above me morally as the moon is distant from the earth.

When the world is crashing to pieces all around you, you can be sure that a handful of your friends, acquaintances, and benefactors will be concerned on your behalf. You should take a good look around before you sink into total despair. If *you* believe that other people are prepared to help you, then they always will.

While I was in the middle of my troubles, a young man called Nishioka Sadataka joined Maruzen Textiles fresh out of school. As a youngster, he didn't know the first thing about business, but he had spirit, he was sharp, and above all he was passionate about his work. He had seen our advertisement in the papers, and I gave him a job the moment I saw how keen he was. "I wanted to get into business, and that's why I came to Senba," he told me.

He quickly mastered the ropes and went to work as a salesman. He never complained about the firm lurching from disaster to disaster but made the rounds of the textile wholesalers and clothing factories of Higashinari and Miyakojima. The modern apparel business was just starting to come into existence, so we did not just sell plain cloth but had begun making it up into clothes to sell to garment wholesalers. Since I had fired the higher-paid, older salesmen, I had to rely on young people with all their natural energy. Luckily for me, they all had big ambitions about what they wanted to achieve in the apparel business.

For my part, I was convinced that property, not textiles, was the business of the future. This conviction grew stronger with every passing day, and my business began to evolve into areas like renting buildings and selling real estate. In 1955, I established Toho Sangyo, an indoor amusement center, thinking it would be a useful business for preserving capital and providing a steady income stream.

I left most of the running of the textiles business to Nishioka and the rest of the dynamic young staff. I promoted Nishioka to head of sales, put him in charge of buying inventory, and soon after appointed him a company director. I've always believed in promoting talent. I'm a man of strong likes and dislikes. If I have an employee who's "got it," I nurture them. On the other hand, if they fail to live up to my expectations, I'm just as quick to fire them.

Ito Zennosuke at the trading giant Marubeni was a man who sent a lot of product our way when times were tough. As the head of Marubeni's textiles division, he took every opportunity to give Maruzen a boost. It's no exaggeration to say that it was thanks to him that Maruzen Textiles did not collapse.

After finally deciding to get serious about investing in real estate, I established a couple of real estate investment vehicles with a group of ten investors, including Matsumoto Yasutaro, a former director of an Umeda textile wholesaler, and my friend Matsumoto Shigeru. The two firms were called Koyukai and Ryoyukai. Matsumoto Yasutaro was chairman; I was his deputy with the title of vice-chairman, but I was actually in control. Matsumoto was domineering, but he always listened to me, if no one else. The other investors were all enormously rich—I was the only one without much money.

Whenever I launch a business, the first question I come to grips with is how much capital I can borrow. As far as I'm concerned, loans are proof of trust, and I treat money that I borrow as I would money of my own. Most people do business on a scale proportionate to their own capital. With that approach you will scrabble away for a long time before developing any critical mass. There is no greater advantage than access to outside capital.

Once a month, the two companies would have a get-together. These were relaxed occasions with cheap packed lunches and alcohol. We were all on friendly terms, and though we were keen to turn a profit, we weren't insanely greedy. The biggest reason for our mellowness was that the investors were not yet aware that there was serious money to be made in real estate.

The two firms delivered better than expected results. As all the participants were well off, the banks trusted us and we could get our hands on as much capital as we liked. The scale of our ventures was enormous, and since every single deal we did was successful, everyone was on cloud nine. At some point, someone suggested that if we kept going as we were, our situation was bound to get complicated. We, therefore, decided to dissolve the partnership, but I am still friendly with all the other investors.

The success of these two partnerships gave my self-confidence a big boost, and I suggested to Hattori Ritsu that we set up a real estate company of our own. She had quit working at Shin-Osaka Tochi when she got married a few years after joining the firm, but I badly needed her administrative talents and her judgment, both far superior to any man's. She was reluctant at first, but finally succumbed in the face of my persistence. "If you have such a high opinion of me," she said, "I suppose I can't very well say no."

In 1964, Hattori Ritsu, Adachi Hisako (my eldest son's wife), and I each put up some money and established Shin-Osaka Jisho, another real estate company. I was president and chairman, Hisako was CEO, and Hattori was a director.

The Tokaido Shinkansen, the bullet-train line between Tokyo and Osaka, was being built for the 1964 Tokyo Olympics. I decided to concentrate my efforts on the area around

Shin-Osaka Station as it was clearly ripe for development. Back then, Shin-Osaka was nothing but farmland. Paddy fields and swampland stretched as far as the eye could see. Caked in mud as we slogged our way along the unpaved roads, Hattori Ritsu and I went to knock on the doors of all the major landowners in the area, lugging a suitcase full of banknotes with us. Although the lack of toilet facilities was a big inconvenience, Hattori, trooper that she is, never uttered a word of complaint.

We bought up more and more parcels of land. I got a bank loan to fund the purchases I was making, but in return, I had to promise the bank that I would get the landowners who sold out to me to put all their proceeds into the bank as time deposits. It was a fabulous deal for the bank: Not only did they get back their money very soon after lending it out, but their customer roster expanded as well.

I negotiated with the landowners face-to-face. "So how about it? I think 1,400 yen per *tsubo* is a pretty good deal. What do you say?"

"Can't you see your way to upping that figure just a little?"

"What? Something like 1,500 yen, say? The market rate's 1,400. That's already quite a stretch for us to pay."

"I'm not interested in selling for less. The wife and I just discussed it."

"You drive a hard bargain. I thought I was supposed to be the hard-nosed businessman here!" I would discreetly flatter the people I was bargaining with. "Okay then, you win. I mean, what choice do I have? Let's do the deal. Oh, and I don't want to make you feel that this is something you *have* to do for me, but I do have one small condition. I've got the bank as my backer, and they'd like you to help yourselves to any cash you need, but put the bulk of it in a three- or five-year time deposit with them."

I had been prepared to pay 1,500 yen per *tsubo* from the

start anyway. It was a fair price, and no one felt shortchanged. More crucial was getting the people who sold to us to willingly deposit the proceeds in the bank that was backing us.

This arrangement made me, the bank, and the farmers happy, too. My policy, as I bought up more and more land around Shin-Osaka Station, could be described as "killing three birds with one stone." The *tsubo* price at the time ranged from over 1,000 yen to 3,000 yen. We hung on to the land we bought for anywhere from several months to several years, before reselling it to either the City of Osaka or Hankyu Railway, which needed to acquire it for the zoning of the new development. Basically, we were doing what's known as land flipping.

The total area of the land we acquired at this time was somewhere close to 1 million square feet. We could sell a plot of land that we had picked up for 10 million yen for 30 million yen a short while later, so we couldn't really help making money. After being operational for only two or three years and financed entirely with other people's money, we had made profits well north of a billion yen. We poured the money back into the construction of rental buildings all around Osaka. I was never one to let my capital lie fallow. My philosophy was to always put my money to work. I think that's what people are referring to when they describe me as "a genuine entrepreneur, not some rich financier."

In addition to the bank, I also turned to people I knew to provide me with the money I needed to buy up land. Takamuro Osamu of Nisho, the bill discounting finance company, was extremely helpful. For some reason, he liked me and completely trusted me. "Mr. Adachi," he would say, "I don't need collateral or anything like that from you. Just write me a promissory note and I'll give you anything up to 1.5 billion yen. I'll charge you lower rates of interest than anyone else, too. All I want is for you to go out there and make a ton of money."

A parcel of land owned by the big shipping company

Nippon Yusen (NYK) in Osaka's Taisho Ward—1,000 *tsubo* complete with a warehouse certificate—came onto the market. It looked so good to me that I approached one of the company directors and worked out a deal, despite not actually having any money. Our negotiations were like a cozy chat over a cup of tea, and I managed to get the land very cheaply by the standards of the day. I borrowed the money for the deposit from Mr. Takamuro, and since Daido Life Insurance took care of the rest of the financing, I got the land without putting in a penny of my own. I took advantage of this opportunity to establish a warehouse business called Yuzen Soko.

I persuaded the sellers at NYK that our using the same character *yu* (the "Y" in NYK) in our name would be a good thing, and so our business was launched with Akai Hiroshi, a warehouse veteran, as CEO. I have since sold off my stock in the company, but I remember this particular piece of real estate with special affection, as its sale later helped me survive a grim period when I had lost a lot of money speculating in art. I was only able to get a loan half the size I had applied for from Nisho, but I am forever grateful to Mr. Takamuro for his kindness.

This is another example of my own style of investing: leveraging the trust people have in me to generate profits with other people's money. Let me give you an example of how I operated. Let's say I heard about a 30-million-yen chunk of real estate. I would quickly decide who I wanted to sell it to and approach them with a proposal. But rather than selling the entire piece of land to this sponsor, I would buy half of it myself. Since I didn't have any money of my own for the purchase, I would borrow the money I needed from my sponsor at a high rate of interest. I would then forget about the land for about a year, and after the value had gone up significantly I would sell it. Considering what I made from the capital gain, the interest charges were a trifle. My sponsor was happy, and I had made a killing with zero capital down.

The secret of success lay in my buying half of the same piece of real estate myself. Your sponsor is likely to feel uncomfortable if you provide him information without putting any skin in the game yourself. If, however, you throw in your lot with his and make a joint purchase, he will be reassured that everything is kosher and aboveboard. I managed to earn a lot of both trust *and* money because I took the trouble to analyze the psychology of people who lend money. Yes, I was a land flipper, but I conducted my business very differently from huge firms that can amass real estate through pure financial muscle. My philosophy has always been to make money in such a way that all the parties involved are happy, and not just me.

That's why I have zero interest in stocks and shares. In fact, I despise them. They're a form of of gambling. If there's one fellow who's over the moon because he's made a killing, there's always another who's wailing and gnashing his teeth over the almighty losses he's racked up. People whose moods move in tandem with stock prices depress me. The recent rise of the stock prices is the result of too much money washing around with nowhere to go. I expect it to all come crashing down to earth soon.

From an outside perspective, my firm seemed to have done a very thorough job buying up all the available land in the Shin-Osaka Station area.

"Mr. Adachi, you must have made a pretty penny by now," the City of Osaka advised me. "But enough's enough. Couldn't you give it a rest now?"

I got the message and withdrew from the market.

When you're buying real estate, it's crucial to go whole hog. If you think your real estate broker has brought you a gem of a property, then you should buy it at roughly the price he demands. That will make the real estate broker happy and persuade him to bring you even better prospects in the future.

Haggling people down to the lowest possible price is a poor business technique. Buying at a somewhat high price and selling for about 10 percent less than the market will win you trust. It's a paradox, but over the long term a moderate degree of greed yields bigger profits than complete selfishness does.

✦ ✦ ✦

Thinking about trust reminds me of an episode from 1971 or '72. Nichibi owned a 168-*tsubo* piece of land in front of Shin-Osaka Station. The Shinki Bus Company, which is headquartered in Himeji, said they wanted to buy 150 *tsubo* of it. I had just opened the Adachi Museum and was looking to Shinki to ferry customers over, so I exchanged contracts with them even though leaving out 18 *tsubo* struck me as a little odd.

A few days later someone in the business approached me. "I want to buy the whole 168 *tsubo*," he said. "Of course, I'll refund you the deposit. And what if I pay 20 percent more than Shinki Bus? Well?"

The conditions he proposed had me drooling. The contract stipulated that I could cancel the deal provided I paid back double the deposit; greedy fellow that I am, I was sorely tempted. When I thought things over more level-headedly, though, I realized that canceling a contract after I had signed it would damage my reputation for trustworthiness. I therefore sold the land to Shinki Bus as per the original agreement. I was left with 18 *tsubo* on my hands, but land values have shot up so dramatically of late that the leftover 18 *tsubo* is now worth more than what I sold the original 150 *tsubo* for!

This piece of land has very recently caught the eye of the Mori Building Company, which is keen to put up an office building on the site. I'm not expecting our negotiations to be straightforward with prices as they are, but I did promise to work with them in a constructive way. I see this as a sign from

God telling me he approves of the way I always put trust above everything else.

❖ ❖ ❖

I have had my share of setbacks in the real estate business as well. A couple of brokers once approached me with a cheap and high-quality piece of real estate they had in Osaka's Sakaisuji district, a very smart and central part of town. When I asked for more details, they informed me that one of the prefectures in Shikoku intended to buy it the next financial year, but wanted me to pay the deposit for them since they didn't have the budget for that this financial year.

The total cost for the land was 140 million yen, but all I needed to do was to rustle up the 10-million-yen deposit. The contract said that I would be reimbursed twice that sum when the sale went through. I made it clear to the brokers that I didn't have all that much money—and certainly not enough to buy the land. They told me not to worry and that everything would be fine. I took them at their word.

The new financial year had begun, and it eventually got to the point where only a few days were left before my deposit would be forfeited. I had not heard a peep about the whole Shikoku business from the real estate brokers. Something smelled fishy. I went to visit their offices only to be told—incredibly— that they had gone off on a jaunt to an Arima hot spring resort. *They had set me up.* Knowing that I was chronically short of capital, they had planned for me to lose my down payment all along.

I was furious to have been played for a patsy. I was prepared to lose my own money, if that was what it would cost to keep them from benefiting from this swindle. Having made up my mind, I swung into action. I went to visit some wealthy people I knew who seemed likely to be able to come up with the necessary cash at a moment's notice. "It's a case of first come, first served," I said, trying to lure them into the deal.

I had to pull everything together in the few days remaining before the term expired. Provided I could raise the remaining 130 million yen on time, I had the right to activate my down payment. The brokers, in other words, would be obligated to sell me the land.

The first person to come up with some cash for me was Tatsuno Hikoichi, president of Tatsuno, the Senba-based textile and real estate conglomerate. A longtime acquaintance of mine, he lived in a handsome old house that had been used as a location in the movie *Sasameyuki*, and was the owner of *Wind in the Pines, Sound of Waves* from Yokoyama Taikan's *Ten Scenes of the Sea* series. (There was great concern about the fate of the painting when Tatsuno's house was destroyed in a fire in July 1988. Fortunately for all art lovers, the picture was unharmed.)

Apparently, this whole down payment incident became something of a legend in the real estate world. People were saying, "Adachi Zenko's been taken for a ride. He's gone and lost his whole deposit."

I did not feel, however, that I had thrown the money away for nothing. There were certainly ways I could get the deposit returned to me, but I was prepared to sacrifice 10 million yen if it meant I could earn a profit down the line. If, on the other hand, the real estate brokers ended up with the deposit, then the whole sum was a write-off. If, however, I got Mr. Tatsuno to be my partner, then I wouldn't have paid the deposit for nothing.

Use it right and money can earn a profit many times your original investment; use it wrong and you might as well be chucking banknotes onto a bonfire. To have won the trust of a wealthy man is an asset beyond all price. Here too I was following my financial philosophy of always putting my money to work for me.

❖ ❖ ❖

Meanwhile, in only his second year as a director of Maruzen Textiles, still my main business at the time, Nishioka Sadataka tendered his resignation. "I want to get into textiles on a bigger scale," he explained. The announcement was a bombshell.

"Listen," I said. "Work is all about people. You're the leader here. You can't just up and leave." I managed to keep Nishioka in the firm for a while, but he had made up his mind and a year later he became independent.

In 1968, his company Marusan, Sumitomo's Sumisho Textiles, and my Maruzen Textiles jointly provided the capital to form Sanzen Trading Company where I was chairman and Nishioka was CEO. That marked my withdrawal from the textile business. Sanzen Trading was performing well, but with changes to the distribution system and consolidation sweeping through the sector, discussions were held with Sumitomo, the giant trading company, and it was decided that it would be better for the long term to fold the company into Sumisho Textiles.

Nishioka was appointed managing director and did a great job heading up the Tokyo branch. He got on very well with Hatasaki Hirotoshi, the CEO of World, and they later teamed up to establish World Textile, where Nishioka is now managing director. Nishioka had a clear vision about the path he wanted to take, and he marched straight down that path with admirable energy and focus.

Both these men, Nishioka and Hatasaki, are now directors of the Adachi Museum of Art. Hatasaki is chair of the board of trustees, while Nishioka is head of the managing committee.

Nishioka introduced me to Hatasaki about ten years ago now. A man of passion and dreams, Hatasaki used fashion as a means to explore beauty and spiritual well-being. A handsome, self-made man, he is also mild-mannered, kind, sincere, and an excellent husband and father. He first visited the Adachi Museum in summer 1982. Apparently he came with quite low expectations and so was enormously impressed the moment he walked in.

"If there's anything I can do to be useful, I'm very happy to help," he offered. I was delighted to see how much he liked the museum. I persuaded him to become chairman of the board of trustees in late 1982, then museum director in April 1983. Life is all about the people you meet—amazing!

❖ ❖ ❖

My attention gradually shifted from real estate to art. Yokoyama Taikan was the painter whose works I collected most avidly in those days. I had bought my first Taikan, *Cuckoo*, in 1957 or 1958—or at least I thought I had. The piece turned out to be a forgery painted by some washed-up artist and not the real thing at all. Even so, I had continued to buy works by Taikan every chance I got. At one time I probably had almost 150 of his paintings, one of the legacies of my more than twenty years as a collector.

Many people believe that wealth should be made up of three classes of assets: cash, real estate, and stocks. But in my case, I have art instead of stocks. For me, collecting modern Japanese art and ceramics was part investment and part hobby.

Apart from Taikan, I chiefly bought works by Takeuchi Seiho, the leading figure in the Kyoto Society; Sakakibara Shiho, who is celebrated for his paintings of flowers and birds; Hashimoto Kansetsu, whose animal paintings are considered unsurpassable; Tomioka Tessai, a master with a truly unique style; Kawai Gyokudo, the landscape painter; Uemura Shoen, a female artist famous for her *bijin-ga* (pictures of beautiful women). The market currently seems to be pricing Sakakibara

Shiho too low—of all the artists above, he's the one most deserving of a price hike.

I started collecting ceramics mostly for investment purposes and acquired pieces by Hamada Shoji that I was sure would increase in value. Over time, though, I lost my taste for his work and sold it all off. I then threw myself into buying up works by just two potters—fellow Yasugi native Kawai Kanjiro and the extraordinary Kitaoji Rosanjin. I love Rosanjin, who was not just a potter but a painter, a fabulous cook, and restaurateur, too. He strikes me as a true genius: Whatever he turned his hand to, he did it at the highest possible level.

Kagami-jishi, a wooden sculpture of a kabuki actor by Hiragushi Denchu, affected me so powerfully that I paid repeated visits to the owner until he agreed to sell it to me. My collection philosophy, however, was not to indiscriminately pick up anything that took my fancy but to focus on masterpieces.

I slowly built up my knowledge by visiting the top dealers in Tokyo's Ginza district or dealers I knew in Osaka for long discussions about art every Sunday. The best dealers cannot get away with any funny business as they live and die by their reputations, which means you can learn a lot from them. The more time I spent with such people, the better I could judge and appreciate art myself. I only associate with dealers of the very first rank.

When I was thinking of buying something, my strategy was to get the gallery to lend me the painting so I could hang it in my room for about a week. This approach generally let me get a sense of its quality. A picture that you want to have taken down after two or three days is no good; whereas, a picture you feel you would happily have up on your wall forever is the kind you want to buy. When I come across a painting I adore, I never haggle over the price. The feeling of adoration is precious in itself—just as a woman worshipped from afar is always doubly attractive—and is at the root of wonderful encounters.

As my art collection expanded, I started to think that it was a waste to have it all locked away in a storehouse. At the same time, I couldn't bear to sell it. And so my idea of building a museum in my hometown began. I decided to make a gift of art—living art and the pleasures of art appreciation—to my hometown. My childhood in Yasugi was tough, but I was raised there. I decided to help the younger generation.

I'm very headstrong. Once I've caught fire, there's no dousing the flames—all engines full speed ahead. Convinced that the locals would be delighted with my museum proposal, I got more and more excited about it. I got a nasty shock when the locals cast themselves as victims, claiming that my project would damage the environment and that I was simply trying to make even more money.

I was blindsided by their reaction. The shock was all the more brutal because I had launched my plan with the best possible intentions. It looked as though the locals were determined to oppose it. I thought about instead establishing the museum in Kaike, a hot spring town nearby, and even met their local representatives for meetings.

Eventually I cooled down and thought things through more calmly. My ancestors were buried in Yasugi, and it was where I had been born and raised. The museum *had* to be there. I made the rounds of everyone in the village to humbly ask for their understanding and cooperation.

In May 1968, two years before the museum opened, I made a formal application for permission to build it to the mayor of Yasugi, Sugihara Kan'ichiro. (Later when Sugihara's term as mayor was over, he became the first chairman of the museum's board of trustees.) I decided to construct the museum next to the house I had been born in. When I stood on the spot, my conviction that this was the right place was reinforced. As there was nothing nearby but the hot springs resort and a load of rice paddies, people were very dubious. "Why there of all places?" they would ask. But as soon as they caught a glimpse of the surrounding landscape they would concede it was the ideal spot.

By then I had already decided to create a museum with two key components: traditional Japanese paintings and a traditional Japanese garden— the mountains that rose layer upon layer far off into the distance would form the ideal backdrop to the garden. The ruins of Toda Castle (the castle of Amago of Unshu) and Kiyomizu-dera, a famous temple, were both close by. If people were still prepared to dismiss the place as an empty patch of countryside in the middle of nowhere, I could always come back at them, "No, you're wrong. There is always the Adachi Museum of Art!"

After frantic visits to all the relevant government offices and local communities, we had an idea of what we wanted to do and started work on building the museum and the gardens. I had visited the garden of Unju-ji temple often as a child and wanted to create something similar. I asked Nakane Kinsaku, a professor at Osaka University of Arts, to design it. The original plan had been for a lawn garden, but we opted for a white gravel and pine garden instead.

After these long and difficult birth pangs, the Adachi Museum of Art opened its doors on November 3, 1970. The total area was 1,000 *tsubo*, while the buildings (the present-day No. 1 Building and the Adachi House) had a floor area of 80 *tsubo*. In those early days, the entrance to the museum was through the garden gate of the Adachi House. The "White House," as I called the original museum building, was modeled on Amago's Toda Castle.

On November 2, the day before the museum opened to the public, we held an official opening ceremony. It was a wonderfully clear and bright autumn day. Many important dignitaries came, including the governor of Shimane Prefecture and the mayor of Yasugi. In addition to the people directly involved in the project, many locals, including schoolchildren, also attended.

I had a strong sense that building the museum had been the right thing to do, but I regretted that my wife, Masako, was not there to witness so many people praying for the museum's success. My tears began to flow. Tragically, she had died on October 24, just ten days before the museum she was so enthusiastic about was due to open. She was sixty-three. Up to my neck in work, I had not paid proper attention to what was going on around me. When I thought of all that I should have done for my wife, I was overcome with emotion.

Profits
from Painting

J ust how greedy can one man be? I think I have a pretty impressive record of hatching moneymaking schemes, but right about the time that I opened the museum—basically the later half of Japan's "high economic growth period"—there was a speculative boom in the art market. The number of good opportunities in real estate had dwindled, so when an art dealer urged me to "get in there and buy everything I could get my hands on," I decided that playing the art market was going to be my next big thing. I lost no time changing my real estate company Shin-Osaka Tochi to an art-dealing firm named Nichibi. I did this in 1971, a year after the museum had opened.

The collection I had assembled for my own pleasure over the years had grown quite large, and I felt that I could exhibit part of it in the museum, while also managing the rest on a commercial basis to earn a tidy profit. The plan was to use Nichibi to indulge my hobby and make money at the same time.

I had suffered plenty of reverses in the course of my long business career, and bitter experience had taught me that there is always a moment of opportunity, a time when there is money to be made. I firmly believe that you should act decisively whenever your sixth sense starts to tingle. Too often a moment's hesitation or indecision had cost me the chance to make a killing. One day, I brought the matter up with Hattori Ritsu, my trusted friend.

"I've tried my luck at all sorts of ways of making money. Some of them turned out well, but most of my ventures failed to turn a profit. I think those failures come from botched timing. Until now, I've bought nothing but traditional Japanese paintings, but if I ignore this boom in Western-style works, I think I'll be passing up a fantastic opportunity. As far as I can see, prices will continue to increase. This looks like a golden investment opportunity to me. What do you think?"

"I'm against it," she said. "There's something about this boom that makes me uneasy. I mean, prices are doubling and tripling so fast. It's like rubbing a magic lantern and getting whatever you want. It all looks a little too good to be true to me."

"That's the whole point, Hattori," I countered. "That's the reason we can make money. We invest 2 billion and cash out at 4 billion. It's as simple as that."

"How much money do you need before you can say 'enough'? You're so greedy. Frankly, I don't care for businesses that don't offer a steady income stream. If you insist on getting into this, then I'll have no choice but to tender my resignation."

"Now, now. Don't say that," I wheedled. "Think about it a bit more carefully. This is a once-in-a-lifetime opportunity. It's not like money grows on trees, is it? Making money is hard work. If we don't make hay while the sun shines, who knows when our next chance will come around? Anyway, money is something you can never have too much of. If—*if*—prices don't rise, we can display the pictures in the museum. Even if we don't make a profit, we'll always have the art." I bulldozed Hattori with sheer obstinacy.

"You go ahead and do whatever you want," she agreed, reluctantly.

I rolled up my sleeves and threw myself into accumulating Western-style paintings by Japanese artists. It made no difference to me if the painters were alive or dead. I didn't care if they were great masters, mid-ranking painters, or up-and-coming hopefuls. If I liked something, I would buy it, regardless of the price.

As a result, an endless stream of art dealers beat a path to the Nichibi office in Osaka. There were probably three groups a day. I rapidly amassed almost 150 works, but that was all according to plan. Since the only thing I discussed with the dealers was price and I bought almost anything they recommended, it was no miracle that I acquired so much in so short a time. But to move beyond exclusively collecting modern Japanese painting was a complete reversal. I borrowed almost my entire war chest from the bank and was so confident that I had got hold of about 2 billion yen.

I started buying paintings in large numbers from 1970 until 1972 or 1973. At the time, the work of nearly all Western-style Japanese painters was skyrocketing. Prices were often doubling in less than a month. Supply could not keep up with demand, and there were stories about painters lining up ten canvases in a row and painting them assembly-line style.

This state of affairs was clearly abnormal. The market had turned into a great big casino, and no one cared about the art itself anymore. As the big trading companies became involved and the banks made low-interest loans left, right, and center, the art world spiraled ever deeper into madness. But the people who were playing the game were so money crazy that they couldn't recognize they were fatally wounded and caught in a trap. Everyone in the art world, including me, had lost touch with reality. My greed was stretched almost to snapping point: All I needed was another year or two, I imagined, and I would have increased my investment to 30 billion yen. Blinded by greed, I could not step out of myself and see how crazily I was behaving.

Prices, however, were rising so fast that I found it disturbing. I bought more works by dead than by living painters. It was hard not to feel cynical at the sight of paintings, the paint not yet dry on the canvas, that living artists had churned out, as if mass-producing them. The stock market was fine—now it was the art market that was being manipulated by a cabal of art dealers.

I bought numerous works by painters like Kishida Ryusei, Yasui Sotaro, Suda Kunitaro, and Kojima Zensaburo. On reflection, it's quite an amazing list, but as I never really liked Western-style Japanese painting, it never excited me all that much. As usual, my passion to invest trumped everything. In the end, I spent a total of 15 billion yen to acquire well more than two hundred paintings.

I had a niggling sense that the work of living artists was dangerous. When small works (canvases that were only about the size of three postcards) by middle-ranking painters were selling for north of 10 million yen, I was much less keen to buy. The flip side of being happy about prices rising was the uncomfortable feeling of "How is this all going to end?" With prices for Japanese art increasing so much, I began to consider investing in good pieces from overseas instead.

To be perfectly honest, though, I was having fun. Western-style painting kept on appreciating as I had expected it would. As I contemplated my collection, which was growing by the day, I occasionally began to wonder when the best time to sell it would be.

In addition to Western-style paintings, I bought contemporary Japanese-style paintings, or what is called *nihonga*. My chief acquisitions were works by Ishimoto Sho and Inohara Taika. I was particularly fond of Ishimoto, and the *Dancing Girls* from his series of nudes is a contemporary masterpiece. No other artist can depict female sensuality so well. He is already very well regarded, but I predict his reputation as an artist will continue to grow.

✣ ✣ ✣

Amid all this excitement, I unexpectedly began picking up a paintbrush for the first time since elementary school. I was seventy-four years old at the time. Since the death of my wife, my sister Yasuko and granddaughter Tokiko lived with, and looked after, me. Seeing Tokiko painting a picture in oils one day, I was overcome by a sudden desire to paint, and I thought back to my childhood when drawing was the only class I liked at school. I decided to practice by copying other paintings. It went well and I was thrilled. I started to copy almost at random the pictures and ceramics around me. It made me feel like a child again. The more I painted, the happier I was.

Right around this time word reached me that *Spotted Cat*, one of Takeuchi Seiho's masterpieces, was to go on display in an exhibition of Japanese paintings in the Soviet Union. I was also told which dealer owned it. Hurrying off to negotiate with him, I got him to promise that he would sell it to me as soon as the exhibition was over. I had secretly had my eye on it for a while already—it is one of my favorite Seihos.

No sooner was the exhibition finished than the dealer turned around and sold it to the Yamatane Museum without so much as a by-your-leave. Naturally enough, I was furious when I heard about this and gave the dealer hell. But it was a done deal, and there was nothing I could do about it. He had only promised it to me verbally and I hadn't made any kind of down payment. The painting was already installed in the Yamatane Museum. I had missed the boat and that was that.

I already felt a healthy sense of rivalry with the Yamatane Museum in Tokyo, and that made their securing of a well-regarded work like *Spotted Cat* doubly upsetting. The Adachi Museum had only just opened at the time, so the Yamatane was better known and had more of a track record. But my ambitions were high and I wanted the Adachi to be Japan's leading museum one day. That is why I couldn't stand it when important works ended up at other institutions. Not much later, *Spotted Cat* was designated an important cultural property—something that just makes my memories of this episode more painful.

I lay in my futon that night unable to get a wink of sleep. I tossed and turned and sighed endlessly. Glancing over at my bedside clock, I saw it was already after two. I had a sudden burst of inspiration. Leaping out of my futon, I woke my sister who slept in the next room.

"I'm going to paint Seiho's *Spotted Cat.* Up you get!"

"Eh? What! Now?"

My sister looked befuddled, but since she knew me well, didn't seem especially surprised; in fact, she was rather blasé. "Here we go again," she was probably thinking as she busied herself in getting the painting things ready.

I am a hasty man and my sister didn't just help me with my painting, but generally took care of

Me with Hattori Ritsu, whose acumen and encouragement were invaluable over the years.

me. We always got on well with one another. She was the perfect assistant and I had to have her there when I was painting a picture. She would squeeze the paint out of the tubes and mix the different pigments to produce the appropriate colors. She did all that because I was completely incapable of mixing colors and had a bad habit of wanting to use colors as they were out of the tube.

"Maybe it's because I'm stupid," I suggested to Yasuko.

"It's got nothing to do with being clever or stupid. You're just plain lazy," she retorted, leaving me at a loss for words. I am the sort of person who's always in such a hurry that I begrudge the time it takes to unlock a door.

I copied a color reproduction of the painting. *Spotted Cat* is a traditional Japanese painting in style, but the medium, unusually, is oils. I copied it in a state of rapt concentration. It took me about a week to complete. I thought it was pretty well done (even if I say so myself), and my sister was as pleased as if she had painted it herself.

"Now that's a nice piece of work," she said.

My painting was the work of an amateur having fun and so didn't compare with the original, but it did have a certain powerful quality, perhaps due to the force of my obsession and determination while painting it. When the madness finally left me, my sister and I ended up having to spend two or three days resting in bed!

Nonetheless, my eyes had been opened to the pleasures of painting, and what with everyone telling me how great I was, I must have pumped out almost two hundred pictures over the next year and a half. Whatever I do, I do with gusto, so it didn't take long for the number of pictures to pile up. I gave away most of them, but a few are on display in the museum cafe now.

Even while painting myself, I was gradually expanding my collection. Every day revolved around painting and acquiring paintings, acquiring paintings and then painting. When it came to contemporary Japanese art, my main nihonga acquisitions were works by Sakakibara Shiho. His *Squirrels in Persimmon Tree* had touched me when I saw it in early 1965. As a painter, Shiho was intensely serious about his work and always aimed high. On top of that, the prices his works were going for—70,000 or 80,000 yen—were ridiculously low. I acquired works by Shiho whenever the chance presented itself and ended up with a collection of nearly a hundred works, second only to my collection of Taikan.

I was also an energetic collector of Tomioka Tessai, who was an extraordinary painter. Unshackled by any particular style or school, his brushstrokes were strong and free. He managed to create his own uniquely serene and ordered world.

Someone once told me that Tessai's *Abe-no-Nakamaro Writing a Nostalgic Poem While Moon-Viewing* was going on show in the gallery of the Daimaru Department Store in Shinsaibashi, so I hurried over. Unfortunately, I was not able to make it on the first day.

"Unfortunate timing," I was told. "It sold literally a few minutes ago."

"But I want that picture. Badly. Tell the gentleman who bought it that I'll pay him 500,000 yen for it. Talk to him and see what you can do."

When the man who had bought it said he was not interested in this offer I became even more persistent. An understanding was reached when I offered 1 million yen. I ended up paying a total of 5.7 million for that painting, but I don't regret my purchase, even at that price. Maybe I'm belaboring the point, but I believe that once you've set your heart on owning a work you should do whatever it takes to acquire it. This is one of the golden rules of collecting.

I was also acquiring *bijin-ga* (pictures of beautiful women) by Uemura Shoen, Ito Shinsui, Kaburagi Kiyokata, and Terajima Shimei; works by painters of the Kyoto Society like Takeuchi Seiho, Hashimoto Kansetsu, and Kikuchi Keigetsu; and the work of Japan Art Institute painters like Mugita Shunso, Shimomura Kanzan, Kobayashi Kokei, and Maeda Seison.

With ceramics, I was chiefly acquiring Hamada Shoji, Kitaoji Rosanjin, and Kawai Kanjiro. To say I bought anything I could lay my hands on would be wrong, but during the boom years I certainly collected a wide range: Japanese paintings, Western-style Japanese paintings, and ceramics.

✦ ✦ ✦

Then came the art market crash. It was probably the Atami Art Fair in spring 1973 that triggered the collapse. Everything lost value. There had certainly been warning signs, but that event marked the point where things suddenly went into reverse.

Living painters, dead painters—it made no difference. Works fell to a third or less of their previous values, so declining by only half or so rated as a quite respectable performance. The most extreme case I can think of was a work that had previously been priced at 10 million yen and then failed to sell at 850,000 yen! I am no stock market expert, but I imagine that only a firm that had gone bankrupt would see its shares fall as heavily as that.

Indeed, the collapse drove many dealers into bankruptcy, and some of them ran away in an effort to escape their debts. Several tens of millions of yen rated as a mild loss, since plenty of the bigger galleries were down to the tune of hundreds of millions. Some collectors even committed suicide. It really was a mess.

I lost 1.5 billion yen as result of the crash, but I managed to survive by selling 500 *tsubo* of land I owned in Osaka as well as some sixty to seventy works of Yokoyama Taikan from my collection—works that should have been displayed in the museum. I knew that I was only getting what I deserved, but that didn't make it any less mortifying.

A short while before the crash, I had told the executive director of Sumisho Textiles, "Don't worry, just buy something—anything. I'll take responsibility if anything goes wrong." I had gotten him to buy a Western-style Japanese painting for 120 million yen. The investment naturally backfired on a gigantic scale, and I started to torment myself about it.

There was nothing in writing, but I wasn't free from responsibility. The trouble was, I had lost many times that amount myself. Did I have an obligation to pay Sumisho the money and take the picture off their hands? It occurred to me that when Sumisho Textiles made money, rather than lost it, no one had ever offered me a share of the profits! This devious reasoning made me feel that I didn't need to take the responsibility after all.

At the same time I was thinking that there was nothing on paper, I'd always been ready to take responsibility for my own decisions. The other party only bought the picture because he trusted me, which means I had to keep my promise. An honest businessman's word is his bond.

Hattori agreed with me wholeheartedly when I told her what I was planning to do. At times of crisis, she was cool, calm, and collected. If she hadn't been at my side to help, I might not have ended up in a position to be writing this autobiography. So I sold off a 500-*tsubo* piece of real estate I owned in Taisho Ward to make up the difference.

Such was the shock of the market collapse that I was miserable for several years after. It preyed on my mind, day and night; I found it difficult to sleep; I lost my appetite. The old proverb about "What's done can't be undone" really came home to me. The herd instinct that sets everyone charging after the same assets is a frightening thing.

Paradoxically, this whole episode only reinforced my faith in Yokoyama Taikan. When I saw how his works held their value, rock steady in the face of general collapse, I liked him even better. "Taikan's not someone you cheat on with impunity," I thought, kicking myself for being so shallow and flighty.

It was then that Hisako, my daughter-in-law and the CEO of Nichibi, became very sick and announced that she wanted to resign. Since it was a health issue, I couldn't stop her. I asked Hattori Ritsu if she would step in as CEO.

"Were the business in good shape," she replied, "I would say no. But I feel responsible because I failed to hold you back when you announced that you were going to go on your art-buying spree. I can't just run away from that."

She was aware that it was not going to be easy, but she accepted. What she said caused a lump to rise in my throat. If I had just listened to what she had said in the beginning, I could have avoided this whole catastrophe. I didn't know how to thank her, so I just sobbed in a rather unseemly way.

"Mr. Chairman," Hattori said to me about this time. "We both need to be careful about our health. Who knows what people will say if they see you looking pale and sickly? Anyone who's lent you money is likely to feel pretty anxious. Someone might well start a rumor that the art market crash has brought you to your knees. Let's stand tall and show our best face to the world." Her advice combined feminine sensitivity and kindliness with a keen sense of how public opinion operates.

I have hired all sorts of people in my time, but I recommend hiring the most able female candidates available and giving them greater and greater responsibility. I have women executives taking an active role at the highest levels of my companies. This, I would like to point out, has nothing to with my being a ladies' man. Women are gentle, flexible, and tough all at the same time—a skill set that's exactly matched to the needs of the age. Most important, they are less politically ambitious than men, which means they are a lot less likely to stab you in the back. For a simple fellow like me, they are a precious resource—far more so than men.

People say that the "Age of Women" is dawning. Women are advancing into a whole range of different professions, often displaying leadership qualities that men do not have. They are more sensitive. Some men criticize women for being indecisive, but men have an endless list of faults, too.

Color photographs of gardens and artwork used by permission of Adachi Museum of Art.

Spring, The White Gravel and Pine Garden.

Spring, The Dry Landscape Garden.

Spring, The Pond Garden.

Spring, The Framed Garden.

Evening, The Dry Landscape Garden.

The "living hanging scroll."

Autumn Leaves *by Yokoyama Taikan (1931).*

Ten Scenes of Mount Fuji *by Yokoyama Taikan.*

Mount Fuji *(1940).*

Mountain after a Shower *(1940).*

Dragon and Mount Fuji *(1940).*

Summer: Four Seasons of Sacred Mount Fuji *(1940).*

Ten Scenes of the Sea *by Yokoyama Taikan.*

Breaking of Dawn.

Autumn: Four Seasons of the Sea.

Summer: Four Seasons of the Sea *(1945).*

Winter: Four Seasons of the Sea.

Monkey *by Hashimoto Kansetsu (1940).*

Fireside *by Takeuchi Seiho (1935).*

Moonlit Evening *by Kawai Gyokudo (1913).*

Green Plums *by Sakakibara Shiho (1918).*

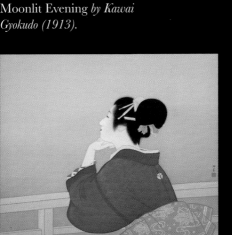

Woman Waiting for the Moon to Rise *by Uemura Shoen (1944).*

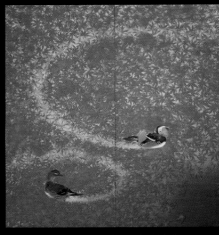

Passion *by Kawabata Ryusui (1934).*

Wang Zhaojun *by Yasuda Yukihiko (1947).*

Beni: Meiji-Period Cosmetic *by Kaburaki Kiyokata (1928).*

Yang Guifei *by Kobayashi Kokei (1951).*

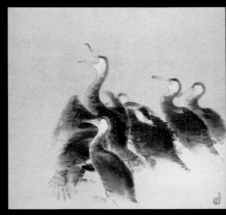

Girls Full of Dreams *by Ito Shinsui (1952).*

Cormorants *by Maeda Seison (1940).*

Tatavana Monastery *by Hirayama Ikuo (1981).*

Three-colored vase by Kawai Kanjiro (1963).

Camellia bowl by Kitaoji Rosanjin (1940).

...wl painted with brush by Kawai (1940).

Angel Taking a Nap *by Hayashi Yoshio (1996).*

Come Again *by Hayashi Yoshio (1985).*

Forest Warden *by Hayashi Yoshio (1997).*

Reading Circle *by Takei Takeo (1972).*

Quartet *by Suzuki Toshio (1970).*

A Backyard Farm *by Kawakami Shiro (date unknown).*

Creating the
Dream Garden

There are two things of which the Adachi Museum of Art can feel proud, not only in a Japanese, but in a global, context. One is its important collection of *nihonga* (traditional Japanese paintings) by Yokoyama Taikan. The other is the museum's 13,000-*tsubo* Japanese garden. That is why we use the slogan *meien to meiga*, which means "great paintings and a great garden."

When I decided to build the museum, I planned to create a Japanese garden to go with it. A beautiful garden is at the root of the Japanese sense of beauty and would be the perfect complement to the Japanese paintings in the museum. When I was just a sixth grader, the sight of the garden at Unju-ji, a nearby temple, had affected me powerfully and left an impression that had lived on in some corner of my mind.

An ancient temple of the Rinzai school, Unju-ji was supposedly built by Emperor Godaigo's tutor, Kakumyosankokushi. It has a dry landscape garden in the *karikomi*, or "clipped plant," style. In springtime, the whole garden is blanketed with azalea, so the locals, who love the place, call it "the azalea temple."

The natural beauty of the local landscape inspired me, but my father's enthusiasm for gardening may have been a more important factor. My father and I had clashed about everything, but as I got older I became more and more like him.

Professor Nakane Kinsaku of the Osaka University of Arts designed the museum's first garden. It consists of a *tsuki-yama rinsen* (hill) garden and a *karesansui* (dry) garden, but it would probably be more accurate to describe the garden as it now stands as being in the Adachi Zenko style. Every since the museum opened, I have been hard at work modifying some part of the garden or other. Its appearance is always changing and not that much of the original design remains anymore.

In November 1980, Hosokawa Ryugen and Tsuchiya Kiyoshi did a live broadcast of an episode of their TV program, *An Informal Chat about Current Events,* from the Juryu-an (a teahouse in the museum grounds that is modeled on the Shokin-tei Teahouse said to have been designed by Kobori Enshu at Katsura Imperial Villa in Kyoto).

Tsuchiya praised the gardens. "The way the distant, middle, and near views merge is magnificent. This place is West Japan's answer to Shugakuin Imperial Villa," he commented, referring to a famous garden in Kyoto.

Hosokawa, who was not one to dish out praise lightly, contemplated the garden with a smile and declared, "The museum and the garden make a good match."

Personally, I am happy when people enjoy my art collection, but their singing the praises of the garden is what truly delights me. I've poured my heart and soul (and my visual sense) into every tree and shrub in it.

Referring to Professor Nakane's plans, I gave workers instructions about where to place the clusters of rocks and the trees and what sort of shape to make the hills until the result was close to the image of the ideal garden that I had in my mind. Raise your eyes just a little and Mount Kachiyama stretches out its bulk before you. Mori, a local warlord, christened it Kachiyama (*kachi* means "victory" and *yama* means "mountain") to commemorate his victory over Amago, a rival warlord, during the Warring States period (1457–1568). Behind Kachiyama looms the summit of Mount Kyorangi, the highest mountain in these parts. It is like a sentry on alert to warn about the changing seasons. Turn a little more and you see Mount Gassan over on the west side of the Iinashi River. My plan was to exploit these vistas to create a Japanese garden on a scale that had never been seen before.

I visited many of the more distinctive Japanese gardens, such as the ones at Nijo Castle, the Sumitomo Residence, and Hashimoto Kansetsu's Hakusasonso, all of which are in Kyoto, to gather ideas. I was given a personal tour of the Sumitomo

Garden, which I thought a particularly marvelous place. I realized that if a garden was well executed, the house in it always looked that much better, too, because the atmosphere was bracing and refreshing. My visits to these famous gardens only stoked the fire of my passion for garden design. Building a garden is an intense experience that becomes more absorbing the more you do it and stimulates your creativity.

When the museum opened, grass lawns were a big part of the garden, but when we enlarged the No. 2 Museum Building in 1972, I decided to create a more authentic Japanese garden. People from relatively close by had flocked to the museum when it was new, but since visitors only really came in the spring and autumn seasons anyway, our admissions figures declined sharply in the second year.

Outside the permanent collection, we held several special exhibitions during these early years. But neither solo exhibitions of Sakakibara Shiho and Yokoyama Taikan, nor an ensemble exhibition of masters of modern Japanese painting worked to push up visitor numbers. We would have been happy with 10,000 people per month, but attendance was stuck at just a few thousand. These disappointing visitor figures were a source of continuous worry for almost ten years after opening. Frankly, I had never expected that managing a museum would be such a challenge.

In any case, it was clear that if things went on like this, we were doomed to fade slowly into poverty. The time had come to make a bold move. I doubled the size of the facility and revamped both the buildings and the garden to make the museum more impressive. I also built a special VIP guest room so that we were ready to receive the emperor if he honored us with a visit. I've always been someone who hated half measures. If you're going to do anything at all, you might as well push boldly forward.

At the beginning, everyone was against my VIP room

Me in the garden; every day there is always some chore to attend to.

plan. "You're never going to get the emperor to come and visit us. You're daydreaming. Don't do it," they warned.

There had certainly never been any discussion about such a visit. I, however, was convinced that it would happen one day. Later, when the National Sports Festival was held in Shimane in 1982, Prince Mikasanomiya visited the museum, followed several years later by Hironomiya, the present crown prince, and Prince and Princess Hitachinomiya. So in the end, my dream came true.

Work started on expanding the No. 2 Building, which included (among other things) adding the VIP room and creating the Dry Landscape Garden. The aim was to have everything ready by July 1973. I plunked myself down in the museum and personally supervised the work with the desire to create a museum that would be recognized as first rate and pull in the crowds accordingly.

With bulldozers and cranes thundering around me, I started a new life: a life where I communed with moss, anguished about rocks, and listened to the whispering of the pines. Sleeping or waking, the garden was the only thing I could think about. When I get excited about something, I completely ignore everything else—that's the way I am. At meal times or in bed, the garden was always there in the back of my mind.

Deep inside me was an unshakable determination to show the world that I would succeed in getting people to come from all over Japan to visit my museum.

❖ ❖ ❖

In mid-June, with only six months to go until the garden was due to be finished, we had a Nichibi company outing. Since the work was on schedule, I thought it would be good for me to relax. The seven staff, including Hattori and Tokiko, and I set off for Wakura Onsen, a hot spring resort on the Noto Peninsula to the north.

This was the first time we had gone on a company outing together, so it was very lively onboard the Raicho Special Express. We were all old friends, and I was chatting and laughing away just as merrily as everyone else. Even so, my thoughts kept returning to the museum. When I closed my eyes, I could see the entire garden and its every detail. I knew the shape of every rock, the spread of the branches of every tree, the progress of the planting of the azaleas—every tree and blade of glass was imprinted on my memory.

I started mulling things over in my head until relaxing into a holiday mood was out of the question. I wanted to get back home as fast as I could to start tinkering. But I couldn't very well leap off a moving train, so I sat there quietly and gazed out at the landscape. Although it had been planned for rest and relaxation purposes, the trip was completely failing. I was in borderline anxiety disorder territory!

After a night in Kanazawa, we boarded the Notoji Express. Everyone else was in high spirits, but I was still rather down in the dumps. Even the smile of which I'm so proud was feeble and miserable.

When the train branched off the main northern line onto the Nanao Line, we began to catch glimpses of the Japan Sea between the mountains. Suddenly the vista opened up and we saw a long avenue of pines running along the base of the peninsula. They were far away, but I could tell they were Japanese red pines with wonderful twisted branches. There were also clumps of the trees on the jutting mountains.

"What fabulous pines!" I sighed the moment I caught sight of them. I *wanted* those pines with an unquenchable passion. I knew they would look magnificent in my garden. My excitement surged to a new high. I asked the conductor what the next station was, then announced to my companions that I would be getting off there.

"Oh, are you not feeling well?" asked Tokiko, who was beside me. She looked at me with mingled surprise and anxiety.

"Nothing like that. I'm going to buy some pine trees."

"And where do you plan to do that?"

"Those pines just now—nice, weren't they?"

"Pines? You mean the ones we just saw out the window?"

"That's right."

"You must be kidding!" said Tokiko, almost at a loss for words.

"You don't find many pines as nice as those. If I don't go and see them now, I know I'll only regret it. I'll go alone if I have to."

And that was how all seven of us ended up piling out of the train at Hakui, the next station, clutching our suitcases. We then piled into three taxis.

"Driver, this may be a bit difficult, but could you take us *over there*?"

"Huh? Over where?"

"You see the pines way over there, right? We want to go there."

With me in the front car, the three taxis headed to where the pines were. It was just after 1 P.M. The driver obviously felt he had picked up a weird bunch of passengers and kept sneaking suspicious glances at me in the rearview mirror.

My heart was thumping with anticipation. I'd like to be able to present this as a fine example of my decisiveness, but really it was more about me being plain selfish. Nobody actually complained, but it was clear from the expressions on their faces that they were none too happy. "Uh-oh, here he goes again," they must have been thinking. But I wasn't going to let that get to me. As far as I was concerned, my garden was my life!

My quest for the pine trees turned into a long, hard slog. As we gazed down at the shoreline or the foot of some far-off mountain, I would point at some pines and tell the driver to "make for them." It was just like a cavalry charge, except that it took us ages to blunder our way to our destination—and once we got there we couldn't very well uproot the pines from the mountainside or the shore that they'd been planted on to preserve. The taxi drivers went around asking the local people who the owners of the mountains were and which gardeners were responsible for the trees, but no one would tell us as we were in a part of the country where the locals didn't know our drivers. And to top it all off, now that I had tracked down the precious pines I had spotted from the train, the reality was disappointing. Some of the trees looked tired and seedy.

We had already knocked on the doors of quite a few houses when night started to fall. Even I was starting to feel a little agitated.

"If it's pine trees you're interested in, then Mr. Shiotani of the Kinsho-en nursery is your man," one local finally responded.

It was as if God himself had spoken. I cheered up, and we headed for Kinsho-en where, at long last, I was able to get my hands on some of the red pines I had been dreaming of. I visited Kinsho-en about ten times over the next three years and brought several hundred pine trees from the Noto Peninsula to the museum garden. The garden now contains around 900 pines (800 of them are red pines, and the remaining 100 are black) to enliven the scenery. All of the red pines come from the Noto Peninsula.

After we had finally tracked down Kinsho-en and the red pines, my staff and I headed for the inn where we were due to stay that night. It was after 9 P.M. by the time we arrived. We were all exhausted from having been cooped up in taxis for so long, and our dinner was stone cold. The trip had turned into a total fiasco. Then somebody piped up, "Well, thanks to you, this has become one holiday I'll not forget in a hurry."

We all burst out laughing—what a great bunch of people!

This is one of the more memorable and chaotic episodes that took place in the course of creating the garden. It's certainly a good illustration of the proverb "Where there's a will, there's a way."

❖ ❖ ❖

When I was working so intently on the Dry Landscape Garden, I would go to Midori, the cafe that overlooks it, plop myself down, and engrave the size and shape of every single tree and shrub onto my mind. Then I would make my way out to the garden where I would try to elevate the real to the level of the ideal.

Beyond the pines, another of the key features of the Dry Landscape Garden is the large, unusually shaped rocks. They come from the Osakabe River, which runs through Niimi in the Chugoku mountains in Okayama Prefecture. The mountains of the Chugoku region in western Honshu are a famous source of rocks. Because of exposure to the elements, they have a dark sheen that gives a garden proper solemnity and weight. We completed the No. 2 Building, which has an area of almost 600 *tsubo,* and the surrounding garden, with its artful arrangement of red pines from Noto and natural rocks from Niimi, in July 1972.

The Kikaku-no-taki waterfall, another highlight of the museum garden, was built in 1978 to mark the museum's eighth anniversary. It was based on the Yokoyama Taikan painting *Waterfall in Nachi*. One fine day in May that year I was inspecting the garden from the lobby the way I like to, when my eye was arrested by Mount Kikaku, which thrusts its way up into the sky to form the focal point of the view of the Dry Landscape Garden. I suddenly had a vision of a waterfall spilling down the face of the mountain. I realized that combining the movement of water with the quivering green of the trees would impart a new tightness to the whole scene.

The serenity of flat surfaces in a pond garden and the vertical movement of a majestic waterfall is a contrast you simply have to have in any serious garden. Nachi-no-taki on the Kii Peninsula in eastern Honshu is one of the most famous and sacred waterfalls in Japan, so I hoped that some of its blessings would rub off on the museum! I immediately got in touch with the owner of Mount Kikaku, explained my plan, and secured his cooperation. Now the sound of water splashing down the mountainside echoes across the nearby fields.

The waterfall is about 50 feet high. It does not have the awe-inspiring majesty of Nachi-no-taki itself, but it is a crucial detail in the garden's overall artistic effect. The sound of falling water in the silence of the countryside has a special solemnity and purity. When the waterfall was complete, Chugoku Denryoku, the local electricity provider, buried the power cables and got rid of some pylons that had been a rather jarring element in the scenery. This, as you might expect, made the view of the garden and beyond that much more beautiful.

The Adachi Museum of Art is just as proud of its White Gravel and Pine Garden as it is of its Dry Landscape Garden. This garden, which is beside the No. 1 Building, is an expression of the beauty found in *Beautiful Pine Beach*, a celebrated painting by Yokoyama Taikan. The instant I saw the work some fifteen years ago, I knew I wanted to make a garden that looked like it—and that is what I have done my best to achieve.

We took great care with the pitch of the hills and the shapes of the pine trees, and also placed the waterfall beyond the pond, all with the aim of imparting fluidity and motion to the whole. The rocks are known as *saji ishi*. I want people to admire the contrast between the green of the different-sized pine trees dotted about the gravel, as well as the pond and the exquisite placing of the *yukimitoro* squat stone lanterns.

I hope that visitors will take the time to appreciate the movement of the Pond Garden and the stillness of the Moss Garden. The Moss Garden was designed by Kojima Saichi, the winner of the first Takuetsu Gino Award, a prize awarded to extraordinarily talented craftspeople by the Ministry of Health, Labour, and Welfare. Kojima sought to introduce variety and modulation to the garden, which he conceived of as an integrated whole. I am proud of the fact that no other garden in Japan offers as much variety of beauty.

✣ ✣ ✣

More than twenty years have passed since I started creating the museum gardens, but I still don't feel completely satisfied. A garden is a living thing. A single maple leaf, the angle of a pine branch, the length of the grass, the way the garden merges with the mountains behind . . . it looks different every single minute of every day. There is something transcendent about it, something that fans the flames of my enthusiasm.

The garden can be quite different in the morning and the afternoon, so it never has the same expression for an entire day. It changes a great deal with the seasons too. Designing and maintaining a garden is similar to arranging flowers in a vase, where everything depends on the balance of high versus low, strong versus weak, foreground versus background.

The mountains behind the garden are like a director working offstage to show off the garden's beauty, or maybe it's more accurate to compare them to an important supporting actor. Depending on the season, they can be half-hidden behind the spring rain, on fire with the colors of autumn, or silent beneath a mantle of snow. Their grandeur far outstrips the power of human artifice. All you can do in response is press your hands together in silent reverence.

The Adachi Museum currently has a staff of five permanent gardeners. You might think watering the garden is a simple task, but even then you have to modify the quantity of water according to the state of the individual trees or the pitch of the lawn. The branches of the pine trees are trimmed and tidied up three times a year, and every single one of the 900 trees is dealt with by hand! When we started creating the garden, I used to personally instruct the gardeners, but now they have all developed a sense of what needs to be done, and the work is more about management and maintenance anyway.

I mingle with visitors so that I can hear what they are saying about the garden, and the members of the Japan Landscape Association come to view it at the best times every year. This sort of feedback fires up my enthusiasm even more.

❖ ❖ ❖

A genuinely magnificent garden soothes the soul. In this dizzyingly fast-paced world, we all need a place where we can escape from the bustle of the city, clear our minds, and be soothed and refreshed. Japanese gardens are places for quiet contemplation, "oases of the mind" with an intimate connection to the Japanese sensibility. They offer a space where you can collect your thoughts and reenergize.

These were the ideas I tried to realize the time I was personally responsible for making a garden for a *chashitsu*, or teahouse. Tsubouchi Toshio of the Kurushima Dockyard Company approached me about helping to design the garden for the Ginsho-tei Teahouse of the Hotel Okudogo in Matsuyama on the island of Shikoku. The building itself used to be the teahouse of the Hisamatsu family, the lords of the old Matsuyama clan.

"Until recently I was so busy with my work that I couldn't appreciate the magic of Japanese gardens," Tsubouchi confessed with a smile. "But now I see that enjoying the tea ceremony with my wife is one way I can equip myself with the knowledge and energy I need to confront the future.

"Business is war. We lose, and the company will collapse, the employees will end up out on the streets. To make sure that never happens I want to make this the best garden in Japan. Contemplating the garden, I'll be able to give my brain a rest. Then I'll be ready to come up with the next big idea."

Tsubouchi was deadly serious. He needed to spend time in silent communion with the garden precisely because he lived such a focused and strenuous life. In my case, being surrounded by marvelous pictures and a beautiful garden gives me great contentment and may be the secret of my good physical health, too. The ideal Japanese garden should be like a beautiful painting where nature and art exist in perfect balance, but it's never easy. Even now, my garden still causes me a lot of grief.

Fifty Years
in Love
with Taikan

Some people refer to the Adachi Museum as the "Taikan Museum" because we own so many important works by Yokoyama Taikan (1868–1958), an artist who left an indelible mark on modern Japanese painting. And it's true that while the Adachi Collection is built on the foundation of modern Japanese painting, it is Yokoyama Taikan who provides the superstructure, in terms both of quality and quantity. I revered Taikan as a great artist for many years, so having his works in the museum is the realization of a long-cherished dream.

His splendor of conception and his powers of expression are incomparable. Taikan always forced himself to take on new challenges, and the power, depth, and structure of his works owe much to his inquiring mind. These qualities explain why he is regarded as the kind of painter who only comes along once every century—nay, once in every three centuries.

That art can bring together a great painter like Taikan and a school dropout like me is an extraordinary thing. But nothing in the world makes me happier than the thought that he and I might have something—an attitude to life, a certain drive—in common, however slight.

I have so many Taikan-related memories. One of these is the way Taikan emerged as my savior when I had taken such a hit in the art market crash. I probably lost around 1.5 billion yen in the bust. I sold my real estate holdings, but the proceeds were far from enough to plug the hole. This was when I thought about my Taikan paintings. Of course, I did not want to part with pictures I had invested so much emotion in acquiring, but need knows no law. So it was with a heavy heart that I sold off seventy of his works—tantamount to almost half my collection—but they raised enough to wipe out my debts. As prices for Western-style Japanese paintings continued plummeting, Taikan alone stood above the fray and maintained his value, which only increased his appeal for me. I decided then that if

South Sea in Darkness, *the great work by Yokoyama Taikan.*

I were going to collect art at all, I would collect only Japanese paintings in the Japanese style.

Right before the market crash, a dealer had brought around Taikan's *South Sea in Darkness* for me to see, advising me to "just buy it and not worry about the price." It is a splendid painting that communicates the full force of Taikan's personality, so I leapt at the chance. But then as word spread that the art market had plummeted, the value of Western-style Japanese paintings plunged. I had a backlog of Western-style Japanese paintings I had agreed to buy but not yet paid for. Despite the falling market, I paid for them all, and then immediately got the dealer to buy them back from me, telling him I was happy to take the current market price. This loss meant I couldn't afford to buy *South Sea in Darkness*, so I returned it very reluctantly.

South Sea in Darkness was later stolen from the dealer's gallery. Although I left no stone unturned in my search for it, I was unable to find any clue as to its whereabouts. I believe that if you ever let a masterpiece slip through your fingers, then you will never get a second chance at it, so I gave up hope.

Seven or eight years later, word reached me that *South Sea in Darkness* was in the possession of the director of a certain lumber company. I was raring to go. By some miracle I had finally tracked down the picture I had searched for so long and hard! Using the dealer who had tipped me off as a go-between, I sent a message to the company director asking him to come and see me.

"Just listen to what I have to say and don't take it in the wrong way," I said to him. "*South Sea in Darkness*, the painting you have in your possession, is not a work that *any* individual should own. Taikan painted it to honor the souls of the fallen soldiers of the Imperial Army of the South when he heard the news of the dreadful defeats they were suffering. Just think of the feeling that went into the work! Surely you agree it ought to be in a museum?

"And the painting is stolen property! Can you hear the groaning of the restless ghosts of the unburied soldiers? No, a painting with such a history is not something that should remain in private hands. I wish you and your family well, but if—just if—you were to suffer some reversal of fortune and had to sell this painting, there is a very good chance you would end up being forced to accept a terribly low price. I propose that you give me your painting and you can help yourself to any one of my Taikans in return. What do you say?"

As I went on, the man's face grew ever more ashen. He had never thought about Taikan's intentions in painting the work, and the knowledge made him frightened and nervous. Nor had he been aware that the picture had been stolen.

"I think I understand," he replied, after some thought. "Given what you've told me, I'm happy to hand the picture over to you."

The man saw my point of view and graciously agreed. And that is the story of how *South Sea in Darkness* found its way back to the Adachi Museum.

The painting symbolizes the souls of the soldiers who had

perished in the southern islands, and the cataclysm then threatening the Japanese homeland. The waves moving toward the shore evoke the American fleet laying siege to Japan; the nebulae in the sky above the palm trees represent the explosions from the suicide attacks of the *kamikaze* special attack squadrons; while the dark, felled tree trunks in the foreground symbolize the corpses of the soldiers who have died in battle.

The vigorous cherry trees and pines that look as if they are about to swamp the cluster of palm trees symbolize "Japan, Land of the Gods," while the mist billowing over the island represents the souls of the soldiers who gave their lives for their country. The brightness on the right expresses the unquenchable spirit of the Japanese fighting man—possibly of Taikan himself. "We may die," it seems to say, "but Japan, our fatherland, is still thriving and will endure."

Taikan's ability to paint a war picture through the medium of a landscape shows the extraordinary nature of his artistic genius. In *The 100 Best Selections of Yokoyama Taikan*, published by the Adachi Museum, the commentary on this work is the only one to have been written by me, rather than one of the museum's curators.

✦ ✦ ✦

I am fond of all the Taikans in my collection, both the major and minor works. If someone asked me which ones I have the best memories of, I would say the paintings I picked up in one fell swoop from the Kitazawa Collection in 1979. They include *Autumn Leaves* and a couple of works from *Ten Scenes of the Sea and Ten Scenes of Mount Fuji*. The Kitazawa Collection, assembled by Kitazawa Kunio, the energetic founder of the Toyo Valve Company, was a wide-ranging collection that included Western-style Japanese painting, ceramics, and artifacts in addition to modern Japanese painting.

The Yokoyama Taikan Exhibition, held in April 1978 in the Maruei Department Store in Nagoya, triggered the Adachi Museum's acquisition of the Kitazawa Collection. The Maruei exhibition featured *Autumn Leaves*, a six-fold screen that is the most sumptuous and brilliantly colorful of all Taikan's works. Tokiko, Hattori, and I were all powerfully affected by the sight of the painting the instant we set foot in the gallery. Of course I knew the work from books, but having the real thing right in front of my eyes made my heart pound. I knew then and there that I had to acquire it by any means possible, so I asked a contact at a newspaper company to find out who the owner was.

Toyo Valve had gone bankrupt and was now in administration. Along with all the company's other assets, the painting now belonged to Mitsui & Co., the administrators of the failed company. The collapse of Toyo Valve led to the "phantom" Kitazawa Collection passing into the hands of the receiver. People in the art world referred to the Kitazawa Collection as the "phantom collection" because it never went out on loan and few people were even allowed to photograph it. Now the finest piece in that very collection was there in front of my eyes; more than that, it was smiling at me and whispering, "Take me, I'm yours." It was truly one chance in a million, the hand of fate at work.

Hattori and I shot off to Tokyo to negotiate with the person in charge at Mitsui & Co., one of Japan's grandest and oldest trading companies.

"We've got more than ten other Taikans in addition to *Autumn Leaves*. Would you like to take those off our hands as well?" he suggested.

His proposal was most welcome. It looked as though I had a good chance of getting all the paintings, but my feelings were torn. At that point, I hadn't yet completely recovered from my recent losses in the art market, and acquiring *Autumn Leaves* alone was already more than enough for me to handle. I

Over time, our facility has truly become known as the leading museum to view Taikan's works.

didn't have the financial resources to buy ten or more Taikans on top of that! Hattori, however, was nonchalance itself when she replied grandly, "We'll be happy to take them all if the price is right."

I was antsy. How the heck was she planning to pay for them? The Mitsui man showed us photos of the other pictures. They were mouthwateringly good. Most of them were important works that Taikan had exhibited in his lifetime. One of them was *Mountain after a Shower* (from *Ten Scenes of the Sea and Ten Scenes of Mount Fuji*), a picture I liked so much that I had even dreamt about it! As I mentioned earlier, I had cut a reproduction of it out of a book, framed it, and gazed at it day after day without ever getting tired of it. The group included *Summer: Four Seasons of the Sea* as well, another highly regarded gem from *Ten Scenes of the Sea and Ten Scenes of Mount Fuji*.

These are true masterpieces, I thought to myself. But how can I raise the money? Having them would boost the Adachi Museum's reputation as *the* Taikan Museum and help us become known throughout the length and breadth of Japan. Wasn't it my lifelong hope to collect and exhibit Taikan's masterpieces? Wasn't he the essence of the Adachi Museum of Art? My heart was pounding with excitement.

When the Yamatane Museum of Art made a stir by successfully snagging 108 works by Hayami Gyoshu from Ataka Industries in 1976, I was still crippled by the body blows I'd gotten from speculating in Western-style Japanese paintings. I can't tell you how frustrated I was. I was keenly aware that every museum needs some high-profile masterpieces in its collection to put itself on the map properly. Whenever you come across a masterpiece, you must seize the moment. It's the same as meeting a new person. If you don't take the opportunity, you're unlikely to get a second chance.

"Are we really okay for the money?" I asked Hattori as we traveled back from Tokyo.

"We can deal with the problem of raising the funds once we get home. It's not like you to be so downbeat. I thought you were the man who had a patent on bold, off-the-cuff decision making. Look, even *I* recognize we don't have a choice here. We have to buy a group of Taikans like this. This sort of opportunity almost never comes knocking. We'll do what we have to to get the money together."

Since crashing and burning in the art market, I had become even more dependent on Hattori. Her thoughtfulness and jolly smile buoyed me. She was also great at calculating and had a vast stock of knowledge on all sorts of matters that I could dip into when necessary.

Over the following year and a half, I paid regular visits to the committee at Mitsui responsible for disposing of the art collection of Toyo Valve. My sole aim in life was to get hold of the Taikans. There was a certain amount of back and forth about price, but we finally reached an agreement more or less at the sum they had specified. We were at the point when the only thing left to do was sign a contract, when out of the blue Mitsui announced that they wanted to exclude two paintings—*Mountain after a Shower* and *Summer*—from the deal.

I was taken aback. "You can't pull something like that

out of the hat at this stage," I countered. "Withdraw those two and the whole deal falls through. It's not what we agreed to." I fought back vigorously, but it was a stalemate. Hattori and Tokiko accompanied me to Tokyo for the showdown.

When it was time for the big meeting, we were ushered into the meeting room. The committee members were all seated in a long row waiting for us. The atmosphere was as tense as a courthouse just before a trial—and we were the defendants. The men sitting opposite us were from the great trading companies of Japan—Mitsui, Nissho Iwai, Marubeni, Itochu. They were literally Japan, Inc. I placed a copy of the museum pamphlet in front of each of them, then sat down with Hattori on my right and Tokiko on my left.

"This is just like the Lockheed trial," I remarked, springing to my feet and trying to calm my jangled nerves by jokingly referring to a recent bribery scandal. "It is wrong to think of this purchase of the Yokoyama Taikans as an issue that's limited to my museum. It's only when a museum acquires, conserves, and exhibits important works like these that they become a living cultural heritage. That is what inspired us to come here to negotiate with you. That is why we accepted the price you specified with a minimum of fuss. We thought you gentlemen understood our stance all along."

I was speaking more and more from the heart.

"Now, suddenly, at this late stage of the game, you tell me we should be prepared to let go of two pictures—*Mountain after a Shower* and *Summer*. These two works have an entirely different meaning from the others. They are memorials painted by Taikan out of his love for Japan, this land of ours. The true value of such works is only realized when they find a home in a museum. I believe it is our duty to ensure that as many people as possible see them. Does anyone disagree with me?"

"Mr. Adachi, you have to understand that there are various factors at work on our side, too," explained one of the committee members, thrown off balance by the fervor of my speech. "It's not that we have any complaints or doubts about your museum."

I protested, aiming for a tear-jerking finale. "Let me explain my position as I see it. I feel like someone who has fallen desperately in love with a beauty, has wooed her for a whole year, paid the pillow money—and now, just when I'm thinking that it's time to climb into bed and do the deed, she runs off and leaves me in the lurch. How could any man stand for that?"

No sooner had I finished than the frowning faces of all the high and mighty folk in front of me burst into loud laughter. The atmosphere, which had been tense and quiet up to that point, suddenly relaxed. And *Mountain after a Shower* and *Summer* were restored to the list, as per the original agreement.

We acquired a total of twenty works by Taikan in this deal. They were *Early Spring, Summer Night, Late Autumn, Winter Evening, Fine Day, Cuckoo, View of Mount Fuji from Miho, Arashiyama, At Midnight, Plum Blossoms, Fine Rain, Twin Pines, Spring Wind and Autumn Rain, Breaking of Dawn, Felicitation* (a work of calligraphy), *Fishing Fires, Mount Fuji, Autumn Leaves,* and *Mountain after a Shower* and *Summer* from *Ten Scenes of the Sea and Ten Scenes of Mount Fuji.* The cost was 800 million yen.

It was an extraordinary amount of money at the time, so the deal got a lot of attention. It was featured in the *Nikkei Shimbun,* the Japanese equivalent of the *Wall Street Journal,* and in *Studio 100,* a program by NHK, the national broadcaster. In retrospect though, I think I got a bargain.

A few days after the big meeting, I happened to bump into one of the committee members. "That jumping into bed business of yours was really something," he told me with a grin. "I've heard quite a few speeches in my time, but that punchline beats them all!" It was a brilliant, once-in-a-lifetime oration, even if I say so myself.

I went on to buy additional works from the former Kitazawa Collection, and never encountered any more problems.

❖ ❖ ❖

How many of the pictures from Taikan's *Ten Scenes of the Sea and Ten Scenes of Mount Fuji* are still in existence? At present, the Adachi Museum has four: the two mentioned above that we acquired from the Kitazawa Collection, plus *Winter* and *Breaking Dawn*, both from the *Sea* series. After I bought the first two, I couldn't stop thinking about the rest of the series. I was ready to go to any lengths to acquire more, but it was a bit of a pipedream. This series is among the most popular of Taikan's works, and pictures from it almost never come onto the open market. Even if one of them does, there's a high probability that it's a forgery.

Such considerations made me that much happier when I acquired *Winter*. Considered a particularly fine example of the *Ten Scenes of the Sea*, it is a work I love and one I had long admired. The painting depicts a calm evening with a crescent moon in the sky above the sea. The crests of the waves gleam and flicker in the moonlight. The depth of the sea as it stretches away from you, the gentle billowing of the waves, the sense of space and grandeur—all conspire to make you feel you are in the middle of the Pacific Ocean. "Only Taikan could do this," I thought with renewed surprise when I studied it.

With *Breaking of Dawn*, a Tokyo dealer approached me rather timidly. "I've—ah—got a painting from the *Ten Scenes of the Sea and Ten Scenes of Mount Fuji* series. . . ." he said and brought it by for me to see. His lack of confidence was infectious, and at first I wasn't very enthusiastic. I knew that nine-tenths of the Taikans out there were forgeries. Why should this time be any different?

Wouldn't it be great if it turned out to be authentic? I

thought. But as I looked at the dealer's uneasy expression, my hopes were hardly high. When we inspected the picture, though, it turned out to be genuine. All of us at the meeting were amazed. The experience again brought home how important whom you know is.

Breaking of Dawn is a peaceful work. A fishing skiff and four sailboats float on the sea early in the morning. The colors of the dawn sky, the sea, and the sandy beach harmonize beautifully. A painting of great delicacy and refinement, it reflects the serenity and clarity of Taikan's spirit as an artist.

I have no idea whether I'll be able to get more works from the *Ten Scenes of the Sea and Ten Scenes of Mount Fuji* series in the future, but the whereabouts of a number of them are known. I would like to get in touch with the owners and try to persuade them that long-term they would be better off in the possession of a museum.

There is one Taikan I didn't manage to buy, a failure that still frustrates me. Entitled *Fragrant Plum Blossoms in Darkness*, it's about 30 inches high. I believe that the asking price was 12.5 million yen. Since I was planning to buy it, I had already taken delivery of it. But the money I'd earmarked for the purchase failed to come through and I had to give it back, grinding my teeth at the thought of what I let slip through my fingers. In short order, the dealer sold it to someone else. I approached them about buying it back when my money finally came in, but they were not interested at any price.

Finding and acquiring a great painting is all about karma. It's not about money. If something good appears, then you've got to buy it straightaway. You have to approach it the same way you would a woman you fancy—without hesitation.

❖ ❖ ❖

The Taikan Special Exhibition Room, which in a way serves

as the "public face" of the Adachi Museum of Art, opened on September 1, 1984. We spent 800 million yen expanding the museum to have a room to permanently display the works of Yokoyama Taikan. It was our response to criticism that despite our nickname of the "Taikan Museum," we did not have that many Taikans on show.

Of the 130 Yokoyama Taikans in the museum's collection, we usually have around 20 or so on display in this room. To keep the paintings in good condition, there are systems like twenty-four-hour climate control inside the display cases and automatic lighting that switches on when people come into the room and turns off when they leave. These systems rank among the most advanced in Japan. "Being able to enjoy the finest paintings in the best possible environment" is my ideal, and I very much hope that visitors to the museum can feel it.

The more you look at Taikan's paintings, the more you love them. Put a picture of his side-by-side with any other painter's, and he soars above them to some different and superior dimension. Aside from the works I've already mentioned in this chapter, my personal favorites are *Mount Fuji*; *Morning of Mountains* and *Evening of Mountains* (a pair of hanging scrolls); and *At Midnight*, an India-ink work. If any works by Taikan come onto the market in the future, I plan to buy them, however much of a struggle it is. Taikan is the love of my life. I never—not even for a second—stop thinking about how I can acquire and exhibit his works.

Memories of Friendships and Reflections on Character

The Adachi Museum of Art has a number of unique features. One of these is the concept of the live hanging scroll, which was made by opening an aperture 52 x 29 inches in the *tokonoma* alcove, putting in a sheet of clear glass, and presenting the garden outside the window as if it were a traditional Japanese landscape painting. Sakaguchi Heibei, honorary president of the Yonago Chamber of Commerce and Industry and since deceased, gave me this idea. The head of one of the San'in region's "big three" families, he founded both San'in Godo Bank and Yonago Shinkin Bank, and served as chairman of San'in Broadcasting, Yonago Takashimaya, and the Yonago Kokusai Hotel. He held a number of other important posts and all in all made a major contribution to the economic and cultural life of Yonago.

I got to know Sakaguchi in the autumn of 1970, when the museum opened. He gave me advice and encouragement about all sorts of things—not just pictures, but also the garden and the museum's interior. We were enjoying a drink together at Kaike Onsen, a hot spring resort, when he came up with the idea of punching a hole in the *tokonoma* to create a living hanging scroll with the garden visible from the entrance of the Adachi Birth House. About six months after the museum had opened we had found the time to get together for a beer at the Tokoen Hotel when Sakaguchi broached the subject in a very roundabout way, grinning and with a glass at his lips.

"Now this is just an idea. A suggestion, nothing more. Smashing a hole through the wall of the alcove in your museum—how does it grab you?"

"Er, sorry, I don't really, ah—"

"Look, sitting on the other side of the wall you've got that splendid garden that you're so proud of and went to so much trouble to create. It would be sitting there, smack in the middle of the alcove, and the visitors would catch sight of it when they came into the museum. I guarantee you they will be astonished.

They won't know what's going on. What do you think? Not half bad, eh? And you won't need to fuss with rotating the alcove picture anymore; nature will do your stage direction for you, morning, noon, and night. It's a great idea. I mean, what more elegant way could there be to show the changing seasons?"

"I see where you're coming from. It's a clever idea. You're saying that we replace the painting or calligraphy you normally have in the *tokonoma* with a real landscape—a living hanging scroll."

The idea reminded me of the way, when I was a child, we used to throw open everything—the front door, the sliding doors, the windows—in the heat of the summer. Looking straight through the house to the garden on the far side had revealed a wholly new and unexpected aspect of its beauty. I thought that there was a risk it would look a little odd, but that it was definitely worth a go.

As soon as I got back to the museum I presented this novel idea to the rest of the staff. They were rabidly against it.

"Making a window in the *tokonoma*?" they chorused. "How absurd!" As for the builder, he wouldn't even give me the time of day. "It's not even worth discussing," he said as he brushed me off. They all seemed to think I'd lost my marbles. I groveled and begged in an effort to get them to change their minds, but it was no use.

But you know me—once I have made up my mind about something there's no stopping me. It was time for action. I pushed my way into the alcove and stood there ready to fend off anyone who tried to interfere.

"Well, I suppose I'm just going to have to do it myself then."

Everyone was horrified, but ignoring them I smashed my way through the wall with a sledgehammer. There was no turning back now! Their only option was to tidy up my handiwork.

The builder looked shell-shocked.

"I've worked on plenty of fancy rooms and houses in my time, but I've never seen anyone hammer their way through the wall of a *tokonoma* before. Takes all sorts to make a world. . . ." The poor man wasn't just surprised, he was dumbfounded.

This is how the famous living hanging scroll of the Adachi Museum of Art took its place in the collection alongside the works of Yokoyama Taikan. The trees, the rocks, and the waterfall of the White Gravel and Pine Garden together compose a view that looks like a landscape painting hanging in just the right spot for the *tokonoma* alcove. We had not consciously designed the garden to achieve this effect, but the landscape fits the alcove so well, you could be forgiven for thinking we had. It is a work of art that Sakaguchi and I, its cocreators, are very proud of.

This was only the beginning; the living picture frame, the pair of hanging scrolls, and the living partition soon followed. Sakaguchi's suggestion was the starting point for it all. I can never thank him enough.

He also did the calligraphy for the stone by the main entrance on which the name of the museum is written. I am proud of his splendid brushwork. He was a busy man, but he would often pop by the museum to ask how things were going, when he had the time. He gave me a lot of advice when I was designing the garden and remodeling the buildings. He loved gardening even more than I do and published a magnificent book of photographs of his own garden.

Sakaguchi would never dream of telling someone else what to do. He was happy to share his knowledge with you, but always made it crystal clear that the final decision belonged to the other party. When you thought over whatever he had said, ninety-nine times out of a hundred, you realized that he was right on target. Some of his advice to me—"Don't do anything speculative" and "Try to do things that help other people more"—made me hang my head in shame.

I'm a bit of a brute, but Sakaguchi never became angry or peevish with me despite the rude and tactless things I must've said. His tolerant attitude encouraged me to discuss my posthumous name with him. I have a reputation as a womanizer and am quite happy to admit that I like women. I, therefore, planned to include the characters 好色—*koshoku*, where the character 色 for "color" has the connotation of "sensuality, lasciviousness, lechery"—in my death name. Sakaguchi, however, promptly proposed substituting the characters 高色, which are pronounced the same but mean something different, with the same kanji 色 for "color" now suggesting something more highbrow.

"Now, you listen to me," he said. "The director of a museum has to maintain his dignity. I want you to hold your tongue and do what I tell you to do."

This was the only time in his life that Sakaguchi bossed me around. After his revision, my posthumous Buddhist name ended up as 美術院高色庭園居士, or *bijutsuin-koshoku-teien-koji*, which means something like "lover of art, color, and gardens."

"Your original idea was too direct and, frankly, a little vulgar and tacky. My version suggests elegant, refined colors. It's much better. After all, the colors in your paintings and your garden are not nasty, tacky things They've got dignity," he explained. "With this change your name is much better."

He was right. The two names were completely different in character. I suddenly felt as though I'd been raised into the ranks of the upper classes. Sakaguchi's insistence on a suitable posthumous name for me was evidence of his warmth and humanity. He did so much for me—and he's going to be there to help me even at the hour of my death!

Some years ago now, Sakaguchi invited my wife and me around to his house to enjoy the sight of the drooping cherry trees in full bloom in his garden. Unluckily, it rained that day.

We ended up having our blossom-viewing party in the reception room, but the trees were still splendid.

When it was time to go, Sakaguchi came out to the street in front to see us off. Later one of his aides told us that the only people he ever accompanied out onto the street when they left were the imperial family and me—that was nice to know.

I once joined Sakaguchi for a drink at his teahouse on Mount Abe. It was just the two of us, so to spice things up he sent for a couple of young geishas. They came and sat beside us. I imagine they were a little older than thirty, the age when women look their best and are in the full, fragrant bloom of their sensuality. One of them turned out to be my favorite type. She was beautiful, petite, and plump and looked exactly like my late wife Masako when she was young. Widower that I was, I was in seventh heaven, but since Sakaguchi was there with me, I could not let myself go. I put my feelings aside and focused on drinking.

I later learned that my eldest son, Tsuneo, who knew my taste in women too well, had given clear instructions to all my friends and acquaintances that they should *never, ever* let me get a glimpse of this particular geisha at any of their parties. Apparently, the last thing he wanted was his elderly dad misbehaving. Sakaguchi, however, was a man of considerable power and influence and Tsuneo could not stop him from having his way. All Tsuneo's precautions went up in smoke. But when I learned of my son's concern, I very reluctantly snuffed out my affection for the girl from a sense of duty to him.

Sakaguchi died in February 1986. He sent word a few days before his death that he wanted to see me, so I hurried back from Osaka, where I was away on business, to visit him in the hospital. He was amazingly energetic, and chatted a great deal, gripping my hand as he laughed and cried. When the doctor came by on his rounds, all of us, including Sakaguchi's wife, had to step out of the room. Once the doctor had moved on, I asked his wife if it would be all right for me to go back in again.

"He's resting right now," she replied. "I think it would be upsetting for him to have to wake up and say goodbye to you. I think you should go."

I knew it would be hard for me to see Sakaguchi cry, so I left the hospital. I never imagined that would be our final parting. . . . I will never forget how sweetly his wife nursed him.

When I went to his wake, I wept uncontrollably. In part my emotional state was because I had lost my son Tsuneo and my old friend Matsumoto Shigeru only a month or so earlier. To lose so many loved ones in so short a time was heartbreaking.

I shall never forget how Sakaguchi fretted as much about my museum as if it belonged to him. "This garden," he always used to say, "is something the whole world should be able to enjoy. We need to target more of our PR at foreign tourists." Raising the international profile of the Adachi Museum of Art is not just a lifelong ambition of my own, but one way I can pay Sakaguchi back for all that he did for me.

His wife is now acting as the director of the Sohokan, a museum where Sakaguchi's collection of dolls is on display, next to Yonago Town Hall. Sakaguchi's aim in putting together the collection was not just to do something he personally enjoyed but also to leave something for posterity. His wife shares the same goal. Naturally, she was very sad for a year or two after her husband died, but I hear that she has perked up a lot recently. "My heart is as pure as running water; my body as peaceful as a floating cloud" is how she describes her present state of mind.

These days I seldom get to see Sakaguchi Heibei, my friend's son, but he has inherited many of his father's important posts and is CEO of Sakaguchi Gomei and director of the Yonago Chamber of Commerce. I am confident he will do his utmost for the local economy.

✢ ✢ ✢

Returning to the subject of calligraphy, the "Adachi Museum" inscription on the gateway of the former museum entrance (in front of my birth house) and the one on the wall of the main museum entrance facing the Moss Garden were both written by the late Tanabe Choemon. The Tanabe family is one of the most famous and ancient families of the Izumo region. As far as ordinary people like me are concerned, they are aristocrats, but Choemon was gracious enough to agree to my request that he do these inscriptions.

It occurs to me that the calligraphy for the Adachi Museum was produced by two people from the families on the "rich list" that had caught my attention when I was an apprentice at the charcoal briquette shop in Osaka. I can only be grateful for my great fortune. It's marvelous that both families have managed to survive and prosper through the Meiji, Taisho, and Showa periods right up to the present day—and I am sure they will continue to thrive in the recently dawned Heisei era, too. I invited representatives from both to the opening ceremony for the museum with the hope that a little of their success will be transmitted to me.

I have tended to fraternize with my social superiors. Socializing with powerful people helps you acquire their way of thinking and gives you access to their networks and connections—and maybe even some of their good luck. In this sense, I always consciously chose the people I was going to associate with. That partly explains why I am friends with plenty of well-regarded VIPs and successful individuals. There are worse things you can do as a young person lacking in resources than depend on the support of powerful people—a valid technique for getting ahead in life and one of the privileges of youth. There's no need to grovel, though. Just because you're young doesn't mean you shouldn't have gumption.

I once had a disastrous experience when trying to cultivate the rich and powerful. It happened more than twenty years
ago. I had heard that Sato Eisaku, the longest-serving prime
minister of Japan, was going to be visiting Matsue. Through
Saito Noboru, the health minister who was an acquaintance of
mine (and Hattori's uncle), I managed to secure a meeting with
the prime minister. Saito himself was an able man who had
restructured the Japanese police force in the days of the black
market immediately after World War II.

When the big day came, I boarded a special train at
Yonago Station, as Saito had told me to. The only people in the
carriage were the prime minister, Saito, and a handful of plain-
clothes security men. Saito was sitting facing the entrance more
or less halfway down the carriage reading a newspaper. The
prime minister was behind him and facing me. Assuming that
the health minister would introduce me to the prime minister, I
started to walk toward him. The prime minister rose slowly to
his feet and acknowledged me with a little bow of his head. I
was so startled that I neglected to bow back and plopped down
in front of the health minister. He, however, did not seem to
have noticed my arrival and continued plowing through his
newspaper in silence. I was too shy to say anything so just sat
silently across from him.

When he finally noticed I was there, all he did was mut-
ter, "Ah, so you turned up." He made no motion to effect an
introduction. The health minister's nickname was "His High-
ness Who Never Smiles," and that more or less sums him up.
Meanwhile, the train had made its way to Matsue. I was never
able to properly introduce myself to the prime minister, and I
never saw him again. Not bowing back at the prime minister
is a gaffe that I remember even now, the embarrassment of a
lifetime. I wanted the earth to open up and swallow me!

Saito was good enough to come and visit me at home,
despite all the demands on his time. He inspected the small

garden on which I had expended so much effort, and my art collection, and praised both. Saito Juro, the son of Saito Noboru,
also eventually became minister of health. He was, in fact, the
youngest person ever to be appointed to this post, hence his
nickname, "the young master."

Sometime in the late 1960s or early 1970s I was honored
with an invitation to Saito Juro's wedding. The matchmaker in
this instance had been Takeshita Noboru, Japan's prime minister as I am writing. We met for the first time at the wedding, and
afterward we saw each other often; I was lucky enough to get to
hear some of the ribald stories for which he is so famous. He is
a jolly man and almost never gets angry. Hearing this inspired
me to have a go at trying to be Mr. Nice Guy myself, but I get
bored easily. I only managed to keep it up for three months.

Once when we were having dinner together, Takeshita
said to me: "Come on, Pops, let's have another drink." I was
flattered and delighted. I felt I had gotten a glimpse of his warm
character, and reflected that often the more important someone
is, the more modest they are. Now that he is the prime minister
and has to look at things from a global perspective, I hope he
will lead Japan wisely.

"Birds of a feather flock together" goes the proverb. And
if you want to fly high in the world, there's no point in associat-
ing only with people at your level. It's important to think and
act beyond any prescribed limits. The secret to making yourself
stronger is to absorb the strength of the people around you—
energy begets energy.

✦ ✦ ✦

We cannot all be moral and intellectual paradigms. But equally,
all of us, whatever kind of people we are, do have our own
strengths. You can reinforce these by absorbing the best qualities of the people around you. Sometimes when I bump into

someone I knew as a young man who seemed to have little hope of rising in the world, they are so radiant and charismatic they don't seem like the same person at all. They had latent talents that the rest of us failed to notice. People who are good at absorbing external influences tend to rise much faster.

Making yourself appealing as a person is crucial. You have to be true to yourself and have a realistic sense of who you are and what your strengths and weaknesses are. You may be very attracted to someone above you socially, but that doesn't mean it will be easy for you to earn his or her trust. Love affairs are not the only emotional one-way street out there.

So what do you need to keep going? You've got to dream big and set your hopes high. An attitude like this will inevitably lead to a wider network of acquaintances and a better sense of what you need to succeed. People who look full of life have an aura that attracts other people.

There are times when plunging recklessly forward energizes you and makes you successful—but you can also end up like the moth who singes its wings by getting too close to the candle flame. Courage and recklessness, after all, are two sides of the same coin. Good judgment is the difference between victory and defeat.

Having a proper sense of time is just as important as being able to sense how other people are feeling. Whenever I have a meeting with someone important, I have always made a point of being punctual. I am careful to arrive ten minutes early for my appointments. No matter how hard up you may be, one thing you can always "keep" is the right time! You must never waste another person's time.

The local people refer to "Adachi time," the practice of arriving ten minutes before the agreed-upon time. If you arrive ten minutes early, there's always the possibility that the other person will be free and that the meeting can start early and go on that much longer. There is also zero risk of causing offense.

I find it very hard to trust people who are careless about punctuality. They seem to me to lack sincerity and seriousness. In my experience, I've certainly never gotten a lot of joy from women who arrived late for a date! I have always told my staff and my family that if nothing else they should always be on time. I was so passionate about this that I would pay bonuses to employees who were punctual, and none to employees who were not. I taught them that time is indeed money!

I always have a notebook with me when I meet people. I jot down different categories of questions in advance—information, advice, and so on. I also prepare a memo of the things I want to say and the order I want to say them in. I think it is basic politeness to cover every point you want to within the available time, and that doing so also creates a positive first impression. When you are dealing with people whose work schedules are broken down on a minute-by-minute basis, showing that you're different from, and better organized than, other people can be the first step in a fruitful relationship.

❖ ❖ ❖

Whenever I went out for a drink with someone on business, I insisted on calling it a day after the first bar. In Japan, businessmen tend to go on from one pub to another, getting more and more drunk, but I have never been to a *nijikai*, or "follow-up party," in my life. No one with any common sense would ever go on a pub crawl.

I'm not saying this because I can't drink alcohol or because I get drunk quickly. I simply think it's a stupid waste of time to string something out for hours and hours. And in case you're wondering, let me add that I do like my liquor: I have a glass of sake every night, regular as clockwork, even now. Alcohol does make people open up to each other, but you can rely on the contents of such barroom conversations. It's best to get all the business talk out of the way before the alcohol comes out and people start getting tipsy.

Some people find it easier to make friends with people over a drink, but I think the best social lubricant is off-color humor. A drink or two coupled with a saucy tale of the things men and women do is the perfect combination—like shredded vegetables with sashimi—and always works. Everybody relaxes and mellows. I don't mean to boast, but few people have researched the art of the dirty story as deeply as me. I fashion my material from a variety of sources: I mix in episodes from my own experience, take stories from the "literature," and embellish stories I've heard from other people.

The long and short of it is that I'm a man with almost zero education. I'm unable to make conversation like many other people. With me, ordinary conversation quickly runs into the ground. And there's only one way out of the hole—an entertaining seminar on the nether regions of the body—a subject in which all mankind shares a common interest. God, I believe, gave the gift of the smutty story as a life tool to help those of his children who are study-challenged.

"Oh Granddad, how can you stare at that centerfold like that? It's *soooo* embarrassing." My "research" often caused my grandchildren to blush with shame on the bullet train. A true master of the ribald tale, however, must be able to rise above embarrassment!

"Some rich society ladies I know are having a get-together. Why don't you entertain 'em with some of your famous dirty jokes?" suggested a friend of mine who was familiar with this side of my character.

I admit I was tempted, but I don't believe this sort of thing should be done in any sort of official capacity. Dirty jokes are fun when they bubble up in the natural course of things, but nobody should feel uncomfortable or as if they are being forced to listen. It's important to find the proper balance between kidding around and the main thrust of the conversation.

The biggest obstacle was the incongruity of the director of an art museum who was also a master of the smutty story. In the end, I had to refuse politely, though reluctantly. Had I accepted the offer, I might have ended up as a nationally acclaimed maestro of the lewd yarn holding forth entertainingly on TV, like a skilled athlete who is wheeled out to explain the mysteries of ball control or doing splits.

There are some secrets to making a dirty story entertaining. You've got to work in some topical theme you know everyone's interested in; the woman in the story must be nubile and sexy so the men will like her. Get these details right and your male listeners will be eating out of your hand. Making the woman too beautiful is a mistake because the whole thing starts to become implausible and the audience loses interest.

Telling a dirty story may seem like a simple thing, but it's extremely difficult to get it pitch-perfect. If it's too explicit, it becomes coarse and leaves a disagreeable impression, so it's important to stop one step short. Inserting yourself into the story and acting it out as if you were in the thick of the action will create a friendly mood and help your audience relax. Mixing in a selection of gestures and movements will also make things more realistic and exciting. A dirty story—precisely because it's dirty—is best when recounted with a light, elegant touch. You can learn a lot from the gestures and delivery of professional entertainers.

Just as in *rakugo* (traditional comic storytelling), the most important thing is to tell stories that culminate in the sort of punch lines that make people roll in the aisles. Make people laugh enough and they will like you. No one should dismiss dirty stories out of hand; everybody has a talent for something. This is mine, and I'm happy with it. If you have wit and humor, your storytelling is guaranteed to be a hit. No one likes a smart ass, but being a good raconteur is an appealing trait and a useful tool.

I used to be hopeless at public speaking. I had no problem with one-on-one conversations, but any even slightly formal gathering would make my tongue seize up in my mouth. It was so bad that I needed a prepared text when I addressed my own employees. I was over fifty before I could speak in front of people without getting nervous. I recommend that everyone study the art of speaking—both the what and the how of it—so they can state their opinion if not confidently, then at least without fear and trembling. And I'd recommend mastering this skill *before* mastering the art of pub crawling.

Musings about Myself and the Adachi Museum

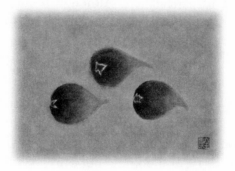

I never really observed any religious beliefs early in my life. As long as I was busy, I was happy. But along the way, something happened that aroused my feelings of reverence toward my ancestors. That something was the way my father Kakuichi lived his life. He eventually died in 1958 at the age of eighty-two. Scrupulous about everything he did, he was a simple, down-to-earth man who was happy doing any kind of work, no matter how boring or repetitive. We had clashed often ever since my childhood, but as we both grew older, we quarreled less.

The year before my father died, he was out in the garden alone, solemnly plucking the seeds, which look like grains of rice, off the Japanese zelkova trees. Looking more closely, I saw that he had filled a quite large wooden barrel to the brim with seeds. Startled, I went out to ask him what he was planning to do with them.

"I'm going to plant them until they grow into seedlings. Then I'll go and transplant them onto the mountainside. After a few decades, they'll grow into fine big trees that my grandchildren can turn to for money, if they ever find themselves in trouble."

I was speechless. Although he was eighty years old, my father was thinking far ahead to the lives of the future generations of his family. He wanted to do his bit to guarantee the prosperity of his descendants. But isn't that what the human race is all about really? Since I had never thought about anyone except myself, I realized that my father was a far better man than I.

I had never once taken my family out for a dinner or to a movie, let alone on a trip somewhere. I had been obsessed with work, work, and nothing but work, 365 days a year. Inspired by my father, I resolved to live life differently. I decided to revere my ancestors and spend time with my family. I wanted everyone to say that I'm a good husband, a good father, and a good granddad. This realization marked a major personal turning point. Not only did I become religious, but my whole attitude toward people gradually started to change.

Tsuneo, my eldest son, died suddenly in late 1985. In Japan, we have a custom of lighting bonfires to speed spirits on their way to the other world, so I decided to set off fireworks for Tsuneo at the first festival of the dead in the summer of the following year. I wanted to summon the spirits of my grandparents, parents, and other ancestors back to this world for a marvelous summer eve-

Finally, I did come to understand what kind of man my father was.

ning fireworks display. If we gave them a show with plenty of big explosions, they would be reassured that the Adachi family was in great economic health.

On the evening on August 15, we set off more than a hundred fireworks on the banks of the Iinashi River. The show lasted half an hour. Since the graves of my ancestors are halfway up a mountain nearby, they were in the perfect spot to watch it. After the first display in 1986, I made it an annual event. The inhabitants of all the surrounding towns look forward to it. At some point, what had started as a private consolation for me turned into a pleasure for many other people, which delighted me.

✦ ✦ ✦

These days I live in a six-tatami-mat room in the Adachi Birth House in the Adachi Museum of Art. It's the building with the latticed external walls, living hanging scroll, and living partition screen. A woman named Mrs. Takahashi comes in to look after me and my daughter-in-law and deal with the daily chores.

My day starts at around 6 A.M. when I get out of bed and offer incense at the family altar. As I close my eyes and chant the names of my ancestors and recently deceased relatives, I see them all in my mind's eye. I go through my prayers every morning, recalling the faces of my grandfather, grandmother, parents, and eldest son. It is a ritual I never fail to observe even when I am away from home. I am not much concerned with the different religious sects. It's my feeling that you don't need any dogma to help you memorialize your own ancestors properly.

After I have paid my respects to my ancestors, I take a stroll around the museum with my daughter-in-law. We go out of the old front gate, then around the back of the museum, along the local stream, for a little less than an hour. We often bump into the local schoolchildren in the course of our walks. Their energetic greetings always put us in a very good mood. A single salutation can influence the whole rhythm of my life; one cheery greeting is enough to make me feel all day that something good is going to happen.

Once I have finished breakfast, I have meetings or sort out business on the phone. The thing I'm all fired up about right now is the building of an international conference center. I'm very busy drawing up plans and trying to muster support for it. Meeting people and discussing things is very stimulating and gives me energy for the next day and the next. I won't stop working as long as I have more than one brain cell left!

After lunch, I take an hour-long nap. I can make myself go to sleep and wake up when I want to. Maybe the state of *satori*, or enlightenment, is something like this. As soon as I've woken up, my mind is firing on all cylinders. That's something that hasn't changed at all with the years.

I have supper at six, followed by a bath, and I'm in bed by

seven. I am sure there are many fine gentlemen out there who find it hard to sleep without the company of their wife or some other beautiful woman, but once you get to my age, you tend to sleep very well without being overly troubled by fantasies or lustful thoughts. Life's easy!

I've been living on the museum grounds for almost four years now. I used to live on the seventh floor of the Nichibi offices in Honmachi in Osaka, meaning I lived and worked in the same place. My life was based in a six-mat and a four-and-a-half-mat room at the back of the office for many years. Chests of drawers and works of art were all crammed in together, so it was easy for me to reach out and pick up whatever I needed. It was not a bad arrangement for an impatient fellow like me. The bathroom, which was less than 1 *tsubo*, contained both the bath and toilet. The bath itself was made of plastic and so tiny that folding myself into it was quite a struggle. The space for washing yourself outside the bath was also on the small side.

People are always asking me whether I live in Ashiya (a smart suburb of Osaka known as "Japan's Beverly Hills"), or if I drive a Rolls Royce. Apparently the whole world is convinced that since I built a museum I must live in some sort of magnificent mansion. They are quite wrong.

"Far from it," I always reply. "Absolutely not. I live a modest life. You'd probably be amazed if you knew."

I have been repeating this stock reply for decades now. That's not to say that I am stingy. It's certainly true that I tend to use odd bits of paper and the backs of fliers rather than proper writing paper, but that's more because I am a poor letter writer!

With regard to food, if I'm going to have a bite, I'd rather have something that's in season. It may cost a little more, but if it tastes good, why not enjoy it? Generally, I eat whatever's put in front of me. I'm grateful for it and don't complain. I am not a gourmet by any means. I'm a big fan of my daughter-in-law's cooking, so I've got nothing to grouse about.

As for transportation, I don't own a car. So it certainly never crossed my mind to get a Rolls Royce! When I need a car, I call for an ordinary taxi. That's the sort of guy I am. I live simply because I learned through personal experience just how miserable extravagance and self-indulgence can make you.

In the early 1950s, I lived in a grand house in Bishoen for a couple of years. The place had an area of 300 *tsubo*, was surrounded by a wall, and had ten rooms. It was very grand with separate facilities for the people who lived upstairs and their servants downstairs. As I explained earlier, the misconduct of one of my employees forced me to give the place up. All I had left was misery, humiliation, and crushing despair. Never before or since has the place that I lived been associated with such awful memories. I decided to never be extravagant about my living arrangements again.

Nobody can predict the ups and downs of life, and pride always goes before a fall. If I was going to spend the money anyway, I realized that it would be far more satisfying to spend it on something that combined my personal tastes and the broader interest of society. My painful experience with that extravagant house was like taking a powerful dose of medicine. This drama of my rise and fall is what originally gave me the idea of building a museum and creating a world-class garden. I'm the sort of person who has to suffer a horrible ordeal before I can figure out what I really want.

On reflection, I can see that my life has been a series of alternating successes and failures. There have been almost no periods of stability and calm, except perhaps these last four or five years. Otherwise, I was constantly tossed about on a stormy emotional sea—from joy to sadness and from sadness to joy— on a cycle of several years. My life was like a seismograph in a major earthquake—more than a magnitude of seven—when the needle is jerking up and down like crazy.

But these repeated setbacks and failures made me into the man I am today. I feel like I grew tougher every time I fell down. The more punishment I took, the stronger I got. I think I finally understand what Yamanaka Shikanosuke, the 16th-century samurai, meant with his prayer: "Grant me seven trials, then eight tribulations."

Many young people today don't think there's a need for them to suffer any hardship other than what's absolutely unavoidable. But even today, it's easy to get left behind if you haven't toughened yourself up mentally. Life is never that easy. If you don't get satisfaction from your work, you'll never enjoy anything.

My present life at the museum is pleasant and restful. I don't wander around the museum as much as I used to; I just eavesdrop through my window, smiling as I hear the visitors exclaim in admiration at this or that feature in the garden.

❖ ❖ ❖

The Adachi Museum of Art has now achieved admissions figures that rank it as one of Japan's top museums, but our first ten years were quite a struggle. I was consistently peeved that our admissions figures never showed the least sign of an uptick. Those early days seem like a different world now. We had worked so hard, I thought. Why's nobody's coming? It feels like only yesterday that I was standing by myself in the deserted museum, sighing my heart out.

At the time, my son Tsuneo and the rest of the museum staff were tearing around the travel agencies and tourist bureaus of Shimane Prefecture in an effort to drum up visitors. Our biggest concern was that Shimane and the neighboring prefecture of Tottori combined had a total population of only 1.4 or 1.5

million. We could never achieve the admissions targets we were hoping for based on a pool of people that small, so we gradually started casting our net wider, mostly down toward Kansai, then Chugoku, Shikoku, Kyushu, Chubu, and Hokuriku (that is, most of western and southern Japan).

The museum wasn't well known back then, so the first thing we did was distribute brochures. Opposite the museum there is a hot spring called Saginoyu. It was popular with local people but not famous enough at the time to attract people from far away. The museum staff wore themselves out visiting all the travel agents, local government offices, and farming cooperatives to ask for their help promoting the museum. All their blood, sweat, and tears gradually started to pay off at some point after 1975.

In those days, I was spending half the month in Osaka and half in Yasugi, but it was brought home to me what an agony waiting for the tide to turn can be. I used to say a silent prayer of thanks every time a group of visitors came to the museum. That gratitude is still there.

There is one man I'd like to single out for the big role he played in the gradual takeoff in admissions. He is Yamashita Kazuaki, the chairman of Oppen Cosmetics. Oppen used the museum garden for a TV commercial they filmed in July 1977. Yamashita had first come to the museum with some of his female employees as part of a training program for the staff in Oppen's Yonago branch office and had been completely bowled over by the garden.

"This place is a perfect fit with Oppen Cosmetics and its ethos of the pursuit of beauty," he had declared, rooted to the spot in the lobby.

He decided then and there to use the garden in a TV commercial for his firm. This commercial proved hugely effective in mobilizing people to come to the museum. It was also the start of my friendship with Yamashita. Incidentally, I was so taken with the uniforms of the Oppen ladies that I got the female staff at the museum to wear the same thing.

✦ ✦ ✦

I'm not proud. I never act the big shot or put on airs. When I go out, I make a point of being humble. If you behave modestly, no one will put obstacles in your way. This is not just true for business. It's an ironclad rule for friendships, too.

Sometimes when I'm in a good mood and wandering through the museum, one of the visitors—someone I don't know from Adam—will pop up and ask if they can have their picture taken with me. I love this. Naturally, I'm particularly pleased when the request comes from a lady, though her boyfriend may be annoyed to hear me say so.

"Have my photo taken with a beautiful woman like you? I assure you, the pleasure's all mine," I reply in a bantering tone.

The photo taken, we smile, shake hands, and say goodbye. I feel wonderfully energized—plus I get to enjoy the illusion that the whole world revolves around me!

"I wouldn't like to think that this is it for us. You must come back again."

I'm an expert at slipping in farewell remarks like this. Often it's the impromptu remarks that communicate the warmth of your character and make an impression on the person you're talking to. A businessman should have more in his repertoire than flowery compliments and abject groveling.

The Takarasiennes, as the beautiful actresses of the Takarazuka all-female theater troupe are called, visit the museum in May every year. It's a joy to be alive at this time of year, when all the azaleas burst into flower. When you no longer respond to sex appeal, then it's all over. You might as well be dead. Show me the law that says it's wrong to fall in love just because you are old! Fear is the greatest enemy of old age. Even now I have a steady stream of dates I keep well away from prying eyes.

I have always believed that seducing a woman is rather like catching a dragonfly. You draw a big circle in front of their eyes, then slowly make this circle smaller until—bam!—you reach out and nab them. Try and grab them without any preamble, and you're guaranteed to be left empty-handed.

The first thing I do is ask her out to dinner. Then I'll send her a little something like a compact as a present. When I feel that the time is ripe, I'll give her an alligator skin handbag or some similar present that goes straight to the heart. Then I tuck right in. Everything comes down to that pivotal moment. You only live once. And with most things you get one shot—and one shot only.

I'm quite demanding when it comes to women, but I did once revert to being a naive little lad unable to push things through to their proper conclusion. It was in 1972 and I was seventy-three years old. Okada Yoshiko, a beautiful actress who had been a big star in her time, came back to Japan after thirty-four years in the Soviet Union. The moment I saw her on TV, I was infatuated.

Ms. Okada was only two or three years younger than I was, but I can't even begin to describe how good-looking she was. Her beauty was so fresh and pure that old age itself seemed to have given up the unequal struggle! On top of it all, she looked proud and noble.

I had lost my wife very recently and had been saying to everyone, half in jest, "If you know any good women out there, please send them my way." Falling in love with someone on TV sounds like the most fanciful thing imaginable, but I had the cheek to say that for me it was Ms. Okada or nothing. I started solemnly telling everyone I met that I had finally found that special someone.

"We're going to have the wedding ceremony at the Imperial

Hotel," I continued. "She's a beautiful woman so I'm going to spend a lot on her."

As I'd expected, everyone responded with the same wide-eyed amazement. "Who on earth is it?" they asked. Their reaction only inspired me to go further.

"Well, let me give you a hint. First, she's a stunning looker. Second, she's the media's favorite topic right now. That's probably enough for you to guess."

After that, it didn't take people long to guess that I was talking about Okada—or that the whole thing was a cock-and-bull story cooked up by yours truly!

But this world of ours is a funny old place full of karmic connections. Right around this time, I was in touch with a Matsuda Motohiro from Kyodo News, the Japanese wire agency. Matsuda was interested in organizing an exhibition of works from the Adachi Museum of Art in the Soviet Union. (This exhibition eventually ended up being called off due to problems on the Soviet side.) The Soviet Union was, of course, like a second home to Okada Yoshiko.

I knew it was a long shot, but it seemed like too good of an opportunity to pass up. "Look," I said to Matsuda. "Since we're going to hold this exhibition in the Soviet Union, don't you think it would be a good idea for me to get advice from Okada Yoshiko who's over in Japan right now? Could you set up a meeting?"

Unlikely things do sometimes happen. In no time at all, it was arranged for me to meet the great lady at a certain cafe in Tokyo.

So it was that I got to meet Ms. Okada. I'd like to be able to describe how ecstatic I was, but unfortunately my memory is a complete and total blank. The only thing I can remember is that I was horribly, horribly nervous, my tongue was paralyzed in my throat, and I couldn't squeeze out even a single joke. As likely as not, I stared at her open-mouthed. It's a pity nobody filmed the encounter so that we could see what kind of spectacle I made of myself.

Still, this was enough to get the ball rolling, and we were able to spend some special time together. We had dinner in Osaka and she even visited the museum. Unfortunately, the day she came it was so hot—and I was so nervous—that I had to bow out and let Hattori Ritsu act as her guide.

Some years later, Ms. Okada made a second visit to the museum. In an interview with the magazine *High Mrs*, she had named the Adachi Museum of Art as "one of the places I most want to visit in all Japan." Naturally, I was thrilled to see her again.

Later, in April 1986, Okada telephoned me to thank me before boarding her plane at Narita Airport. She didn't want a crowd and had a quiet send-off with only one person—the actress Sugimura Haruko—to see her on her way.

"The press conference is over and I'm heading back to the Soviet Union now. I will probably never set foot in Japan again. Thank you for all you did for me while I was here. I do hope you will come and visit me."

She was too kind. I felt deeply moved.

"Do your best to serve as a bridge to bring Japan and the Soviet Union closer," I answered, giving her encouragement even as I said goodbye. I count this among the most unforgettable experiences of my "youth."

❖ ❖ ❖

Nothing makes me happier than people telling me how fabulous the museum is and generally showering me with praise. It makes me feel that building the museum was the right thing to do.

"People shouldn't come to a place like this just once in a year. They should come often and feel purified, uplifted, and

refreshed with each visit. Frankly, at 1,500 yen it's a bargain."
When a museum visitor says something like that to me, I want
to seize her hand, kiss it, and tell her that I am completely at
her service.

In the days when other museums cost 500 yen, the Adachi
Museum already cost 1,000. Our entrance charge now is 1,500
yen. Some people think it's too much, but I disagree. These
days it costs 2,000 yen to see a movie. But here, you can relax
for a whole day if you want to, enjoying the art and the peace
and quiet of the garden. It certainly isn't expensive if you think
of it in those terms.

It's a mistake to be too quick to look at emotional satisfaction in financial terms. The Japanese have a bad habit of judg-
ing things by their price. How much is this? How much is that?
This is not a good trait; I'd like to see a lot less of it.

Some bean-counter types make the case that now that we
have lots of visitors we should drop the price. I argue the opposite. They see the entrance charge as one part of a profit-mak-
ing business, but I see it as a donation that will go to pay for the
museum's running costs and for new acquisitions.

Some people may not like it if I compare the admission
fee to the money offerings made at shrines, but I think it's only
natural for people to feel grateful when someone has shown
them something beautiful. If people can accept that, then I
think they can understand why I choose to see it as a donation.

In my wanderings around the museum, from time to time
I pop into one of the two teahouses, Juryu-an or Juraku-an, and
ask for the tea ceremony. I've always been hopeless at these sorts
of formal occasions and can never fully relax. I always squirm
when people praise the teahouses, saying things like, "Oh, how
splendid to have a place where you can meditate." I feel so awkward that I have to slip away. The fact that I haven't developed
proper poetic tastes despite an oversupply of teahouses literally
in my backyard shows that I was born with work, work, and

nothing but work on the brain—a common enough side effect of being born poor, I suppose.

At the time of writing, the Adachi Museum has been operating for nineteen years without a single holiday. I believe that we must never disappoint any of our visitors, many of whom come from far away. I am confident that the staff are as polite and well-drilled as that of any other gallery. And in addition to modern Japanese paintings and the Japanese garden, the museum also offers teahouses, gold-leaf lacquerware, modern ceramics, illustrations from children's books, and sculpture.

Ultimately, museums are a form of cultural enterprise in which the state should take a leading role. Those of us with private museums are standing in for the government in a way. This philosophy inspired me to apply for funds from the Development Bank of Japan once. Since it is a government-owned bank, it had not yet loaned money to a museum, but I managed to persuade Hirata Keichiro, the president, when he came to visit us.

"Look at me. Here I am, a puny weakling, shouldering a task that by rights the government should be taking care of. I am doing something that benefits the country. What can possibly be wrong with the government giving me a loan?"

As a result, we received Japan's first-ever state loan to a museum. It was classified as "investment in regional development" and had a term of fifteen years. I was delighted that the government had seen my point of view and given us their seal of approval.

I did not create this place by myself. This museum was established and now operates with donations from many individuals and companies (particularly my own). The Adachi Museum of Art is like a crystal formed from many votive offerings. That is one reason I think of the entrance fee as a donation. I hope you can understand.

What's in
a Name?

I am a little shy to admit it, but I think that I have evolved as a person since I opened the museum. I started thinking seriously about the whole issue of "giving back" to society. As much as I can, I want to try and repay society for the good fortune I have enjoyed. This desire is only getting stronger with the passing years.

In winter 1977, I invited Kohata Shusuke, vice president and director of the *San'in Chuo Shinpo* newspaper, to dinner at Tamatsukuri Onsen, not too far to the west of here. The dinner was really just a pretext to talk to him about my plan to produce drawings for charity. Back when Shusuke's father, Kohata Kyuemon, had been head of the firm, he had done an enormous amount to help us with the museum, so I was keen to become friends with his son.

A wonderful array of food was spread on the table before us. I slowly undid the knot of my *furoshiki* cloth wrapper and pulled out a sheet of paper. On this I drew an eggplant with a squeaky magic marker.

"Hmm . . . You're obviously quite an expert."

The drawing wasn't really good enough to show anybody, but Kohata expressed his admiration chiefly out of good manners. Not paying too much attention, I launched into an explanation of my plan. "I want to sell my drawings to visitors to the museum for 1,200 yen each. Deducting the cost of the materials, I'll be able to give 1,000 yen per drawing to charity. What do you think?"

"You're—ah—planning to *sell* that drawing?"

"That's right. And I want to donate the proceeds to charity."

"A very noble plan," he responded automatically, but it was written on his face that he thought no one in their right mind would pay 1,200 yen for a mere doodle like that. And he was right: The picture was obviously the work of an amateur.

I soldiered on regardless.

"I'm not talking about selling just a hundred or a thousand of these. I'm planning to draw *ten thousand* of them so I can make a final donation of 10 million yen."

The expression on Kohata's face was now one of utter disbelief, and his response a series of vague, noncommittal grunts. That was par for the course. After all, ten thousand was a pretty fantastic figure. Even if I worked at the rate of ten drawings a day, I would still need three years to finish. I could see why Kohata was finding it hard to take me seriously.

A man has to keep his word, so I started drawing madly before and after meals, in intervals of work, cutting back on my sleep. I kept my magic marker with me even when I had meetings. With drawing, being good or bad isn't important. It's about communicating feeling. And that's what charity's all about, too.

The actual business of drawing proved to be difficult. At the beginning, it was a real battle as my eggplants came out looking like dishcloth gourds or pumpkins. I was so tense that the lines didn't come out on paper the way I planned and my back soon started hurting. Clearly, I was directing my energy in the wrong way.

Despite these false starts, I finally got the hang of it after a certain point. Once I had passed the thousand mark, everything was plain sailing. I even started thinking that eggplants by themselves were a bit sad, so I began adding little gnomic inscriptions like "One Mount Fuji, two hawks, and three eggplants" and "The lessons your parents teach you and the flower of the eggplant are always benign."

To produce a hundred of these was a tough task that took me a whole day, from early morning to late at night. Still, I've always been a big believer in hard work and good customer service, so I didn't mind.

When I got up to around the two thousand mark, I suddenly got bogged down and things became much more difficult.

I had breathed in so much of the thinner from the magic marker that I lost my sense of smell. I felt weak and nauseated and even began muttering about throwing in the towel. Things had gotten so bad that I couldn't stand the sight of eggplants!

However, the memory of the incredulous expression on Kohata's face and the thought of all the people who had already bought my inept drawings made me feel ashamed of my weakness. Pulling myself together, I put my nose back to the grindstone.

Perhaps because I was now truly determined to see the thing through, I got into a rhythm and found the work much easier. After four thousand, I could draw the pictures with my eyes shut. They came out so much alike that I might have been making photocopies. The essence of folk craft is to eliminate any waste and uncover the beauty inherent in the skill of the craftsman. I felt I was beginning to grasp this truth.

From time to time I would get a supportive phone call from Kohata. "How's it going?" he would ask, but there was an undercurrent in his voice suggesting he didn't believe I could ever sell ten thousand of the things. His tone was lighthearted, as if he were ringing up to wish me routine compliments of the season, but I was spending every moment of every day with a magic marker in my hand.

I should explain why I was so enthusiastic about drawing eggplants. First, the eggplant is one of the most long-lived of vegetables. It can flower even in December, and when it flowers it always yields fruit. Second, it's a thoroughly wholesome vegetable that does no one any harm. Third, there are few other foods that can be turned into so many dishes.

Eggplant is delicious when pickled, and tasty as tempura. You can boil it and fry it. It goes very well with *tsuyu* dipping sauce. It is the king of vegetables and has a host of positive associations. That's the reason I always draw eggplants when people ask me to draw something.

Thinking about eggplants reminds me of the time Saka-moto Shigetoshi, the CEO of Hoshizaki Electric and a very friendly man, came to the museum. When I asked him to think of an inscription to go beside my picture of an eggplant, he immediately came up with this.

A girl of eighteen,
The first sip
Of even coarse brown tea
Tastes good.
Dark and flawless,
With wonderful skin,
She tastes so good
I won't be sharing her
With anyone.

There's an old line about the perfect whiteness of a woman's skin, but Sakamoto turned this on its head, since the darker an eggplant is the better. To come up with something this good off the cuff was quite a display of wit and ingenuity. I'm not surprised that Sakamoto's nickname is the "Matsushita Konosuke of Shimane Prefecture," a reference to the legendary founder of Panasonic. In addition to inventing and commercializing electronic devices, Sakamoto is a cultivated man who has written about local politics and government reform.

He first came to the museum two years after it opened and was a fan of the *bijin-ga* (pictures of beautiful women) of Ito Shinsui, a celebrated master of the genre.

"I'd really like to buy one off you," he said.

So I sold him one. He is actually quite a fine painter himself.

In autumn 1978, around six months after we had announced the fundraising drive and started selling the egg-plant drawings in the museum shop, a group of journalists dropped into the museum to enjoy the fall colors after visiting the nearby Kiyomizu-dera temple. They all belonged to a club for the managers of media companies headquartered or with branch offices in Matsue. Kohata was with them.

We were getting the people who bought my drawings to write their names and addresses in a register. By this time, we already had more than five thousand people on the list. Kohata was astonished, and when he got back to his office he immediately had the necessary preparations made so the company could accept the 10 million yen I had promised him.

In summer 1979 I presented *San'in Chuo Shinpo* with the 10 million yen I had raised by selling my drawings. The firm had taken the necessary steps to set up a social contribution division and my 10 million yen was the first donation they received.

The first five thousand drawings sold were a little on the clumsy side, so I consulted the register to send all the early buyers free tickets to the museum.

I probably ended up drawing around fifteen thousand eggplant pictures altogether. At first, I'd thought it would take me three years, but I managed to polish them all off in two. I also reached my financial target. It just goes once again to show that you can achieve anything if you really put your mind to it.

✵ ✵ ✵

We sent out complimentary tickets to 12,500 local households (five tickets per family) in Yasugi and Nogi between February 1 and March 20, 1988, as an expression of gratitude for their support. I had the idea because over the years I had noticed that the local people, precisely because they lived so close, never seemed to get around to visiting the museum. The promotion worked. Many locals came and were able to renew their relationship with us.

"I'm surprised. This is the first time I've been here in five

I took up the challenge of producing ten thousand drawings for charity.

years, and it's completely changed from my last visit," commented one man who brought his family with him. "Last time I was here I had a good look around and thought it was an amazing place, but it's gotten even better. Thank you all so much. I know my family and I will enjoy ourselves today." His appreciative comments, relayed to me by one of the museum staff, brought tears to my eyes.

No business can succeed without the support of the local people; you have to engage with the people in your region. Most of the museum staff I employ were born locally. Employees are one of the most precious assets of any business, so treating the local people with respect is a crucial first step to establishing a business.

As a boy, I was dirt-poor and not too brainy, but after more than half a century I was lucky enough to be able to return to the place I was born and create my own museum. This was something I never expected to be able to do, and I was so focused on trying to build a museum I could be proud of that I didn't have time to enjoy it at first. Only once the enterprise had gotten more or less onto an even keel could I afford to look around and take stock.

We held a Yokoyama Taikan exhibition in October 1980 to

mark the museum's tenth anniversary, making use of the museum's entire exhibition space to show more than seventy of his works. On October 1, we invited around four hundred prominent people from Tokyo, Osaka, and the local area to a commemoration ceremony. I was delighted that almost everyone we invited took time out from their busy schedules to attend.

Early in the morning, everyone assembled outside the museum entrance for a ribbon-cutting ceremony with the director of the Agency for Cultural Affairs and Yokoyama Takashi of the Yokoyama Taikan Memorial Hall doing the honors. Then a statue of me by the sculptor Kitamura Seibo was unveiled. I love daytime fireworks, so we let off some of these. We had also planned to release eighty-two birds (my age at the time) into the sky, but they were so frightened by the noise of the fireworks they refused to come out of their cage! What a shame. After the ceremony, we went to Yasugi for a party. I got the film director Okamoto Kihachi, a distant relative of mine, to record the event.

These days, the Adachi Museum is known throughout Japan. Several members of the imperial family—Prince Hironomiya (now Crown Prince Naruhito), Prince and Princess Hitachinomiya, and Prince Mikasanomiya—have visited the museum and enjoyed its serene atmosphere, and in so doing fulfilled a dream I have had since opening the place. We have also had many important visitors from overseas, including figures from the art world such as Jan Fontein, the director of the Boston Museum of Fine Arts.

Of course, I couldn't have done any of this without the support of the local people. The most basic elements of the museum—the land where the museum, garden, and parking lot stand—I got from the local people. It is only right for me to feel intensely thankful.

People have always thought of me as a mover and shaker. I think I have successfully combined success in business with having few enemies because I've managed to find a balance between greed and good nature. My name, Zenko, which means "good deeds," has had an influence, making me eager to do good, though not in a showy style. Once you're my age, you're not interested in showing off. I act according to my feelings. I am too old to get any satisfaction from being self-centered.

✧ ✧ ✧

During the time I was compiling this book, I went into the hospital for a major operation. Not wanting to make a fuss about it, I didn't tell anyone outside of a handful of the people closest to me. But as water always sinks into the ground, word seeped into the neighborhood and my secret came out. Let me tell you a little about that episode.

At the beginning of February 1988, I had my regular check-up from my doctor, a general practitioner and the director of the Kawamura Hospital in Hirose.

"I've found something a little worrying," he said. "Tomorrow I'd like to do a cardiogram and some X-rays."

I hadn't noticed anything wrong. I felt fine, so I agreed cheerfully and without any anxiety.

"You have some kind of shadow in your lung," I was told after my tests in the hospital the next day. "We think more detailed tests are necessary. We would like you to go into a general hospital."

My birthday was just around the corner, and I knew the family back at home was planning something, but I've always been an impatient fellow. If I had to go to a hospital, then sooner was better than later. I checked myself into the National Yonago Hospital on February 8, my birthday, thinking this might bring me good luck.

This was only my third time in the hospital in my ninety-

Pointing the way . . . Sculpture by Kitamura Seibo.

year life. The first time was three years ago, when I'd fallen over on my back and hurt my spine while putting in some eyes drops; the second time was for an inner-ear inflammation; and now this. The first two times had been for simple, childish problems, so this *felt* like the first time to me.

In the hospital I was put through a barrage of complex tests—X-rays, measurements of my blood sedimentation rate and blood pressure, and so on—every day for almost a month. I had never expected things to take quite so long, but with two young nurses for me to flirt with, I never got bored. I have the gift of being able to be content no matter where I am. In particular, when it comes to women I have a highly developed talent for being hopeful, regardless of my age.

The results of the tests were not the greatest and the doctors decided that I needed an operation. My family told me I had something called geriatric tuberculosis of the lung. I had never dreamed that I would end up needing an operation, so the news gave me quite a fright.

"There's really no need to worry, Mr. Adachi," said Dr. Ikeda Mitsugu, the physician in charge and a cheery, witty man. "Besides, I hear your nickname is 'phoenix.' So I'm sure you'll get the better of your sickness and send it on its way with its tail between its legs."

Dr. Ikeda would always pop in to see me in the morning and evening to tell me a little gossip or a funny story. As you can imagine, this was a great help in calming my nerves.

"Never had a patient as full of beans as this one . . . " said the nurses, "or quite as feisty."

They would give my hand a good squeeze back whenever I reached out to grab theirs and were very supportive. I was full of admiration for their cheerfulness and commitment. They would take turns checking up on me and asking, "And how are we today, Mr. Adachi?"—a little routine that made me very happy. To me, they looked like goddesses. In fact, I found the sight of their brisk, competent movements deeply reassuring. Having never had an operation in my life, I pretended to be relaxed on the outside, while on the inside I was terrified. Despite my assertive nature, I'm a coward.

My daughter-in-law was at my side the whole time. My grandchildren also rushed to support me, but the sight of their faces around my bed ended up depressing me. Mr. Hatasaki, director of the museum trustees, came by. I started tormenting myself with all sorts of imaginary fears: Perhaps my illness was really serious? I mean, could I *really* be having an operation for tuberculosis at the age of ninety? It was hard to believe. I started worrying that lung cancer was really the problem.

"Doctor, does a man of ninety have the strength to survive an operation for lung cancer?" I asked.

"Now, nobody ever *said* it was lung cancer, did they?" Dr. Ikeda responded.

"Well, you're the expert, not me, so whatever you say. But has anyone else over eighty years old in Japan had this operation?"

"Oh yes, five or six people."

"How confident are you then?"

"Very. If I weren't, I wouldn't be operating. Don't worry. Just trust me."

"If that's what you think, then I'm happy to leave everything up to you, doctor. Let's do it."

I decided to go ahead with the operation, putting complete faith in the doctor.

The day before the operation the doctor came to my room with a sleeping pill for me. He knew that plenty of people were too nervous to sleep the night before an operation. But I had already made up my mind.

"Doctor, I won't be needing any sleeping pills, but just let me go to sleep earlier than usual, at 6 P.M." I said, showing him that I was not afraid.

The result of this bravado was that Dr. Ikeda got nervous instead and had to take a sleeping pill that night—even doctors are human like the rest of us! Later someone told me that Dr. Ikeda had discussed my case with his father, a general practitioner in Okinoshima, who had told him that operating on a ninety-year old was too dangerous and he shouldn't do it. That advice must have rattled him even more.

My grandson, Takanori, came to see me. "Don't you worry," he told me, an earnest expression on his face. "Everything's going to be fine. I went to see a fortune-teller. She said that Adachi Zenko is a wonderfully lucky name—one-in-a-hundred-thousand-people sort of lucky—and guaranteed that you'll just get luckier and luckier the longer you live. Apparently, you're destined to live past a hundred."

I really appreciated Takanori's thoughtfulness at such a time. Although he can seem a little standoffish, he is a kind lad underneath. When he was a boy, he was very ill-mannered and would walk off instead of greeting visitors properly. He sometimes reminds me about the time I became so annoyed that I chased him down the road with a hammer! Anyway, I hope Takanori will do a great job as the director of the Adachi Museum.

His sister, Tokiko, works as a curator at the museum. Back when she was in fifth grade and running for vice-chair of the student council, I made her practice her speech so many times she ended up in tears—though she did master it. I hope this taught her that persistence always pays off.

I took Tokiko to commercial galleries with me from an early age so she could learn about buying paintings. I developed her market savvy by getting her to write her estimate of a painting's price on a scrap of paper and then comparing it with the figure Hattori and I had come up with.

It's easy to spoil your children and grandchildren—they are family after all—but the fact that they're family should not make you overly gentle. "Spare the rod and spoil the child" goes the proverb. I believe in tough love.

The day after Takanori had shared the fortuneteller's encouraging verdict, I went into the operating theater with many members of my family looking on. The operation began at 8:30 A.M. and lasted until 1:30 P.M., five hours altogether. Since I was under an anesthetic, I remember nothing, but I did have a couple of very bizarre dreams. In one of them, I had been put on the operating table without any anesthetic and was quite desperate to escape. I was later told that I had in fact been writhing around so madly that it took several doctors to hold me down. My strength was not that of a normal ninety-year-old.

In the other dream I was slowly sucked down into a deep, bowl-shaped valley where thousands upon thousands of dead leaves were whirling around in the wind. A darkness, like a huge and mighty whirlpool, was sucking me and everything else down. It was a vision of hell. I desperately tried to escape, but there was nothing I could do. As the circling coils became smaller and smaller, they went around faster and faster; at the moment when I was about to be sucked into the mouth of hell, my eyes snapped open.

"It was a success. The operation's over, and it went fine."

I was drenched with sweat. I had no memory of the operation. My heart was still pounding with terror from my dream.

All I could think was "I'm safe."

I was taken back to the ward where I recounted my dream to Hisako. "It could have been because of the anesthetic," she suggested. "When the anesthetic starts to work and again when it wears off, you often have dreams where you float away and lose consciousness. They're different from normal dreams." She probably knew this because she had been very sick herself in the past. Now she's 100 percent better and takes great care of me. We enjoy talking and she makes wonderful dishes for me every day—all-in-all a much better daughter-in-law than I deserve.

"I hope I never have dreams like that again," I said.

"You never know, they might have been lucky. If you'd not regained consciousness—now that would be something worth complaining about! It just shows what a powerful will to live you've got."

"Perhaps—no, you're definitely right. The dream was a message telling me to live life more fully, a test to see just how much I wanted to live."

I recovered rapidly and congratulated myself on having beaten the disease. The fact that I had been successfully operated on for lung cancer at the age of ninety boosted my mood.

The doctor dropped by to tell me that the operation had gone perfectly. The diseased part of my lung had been protruding from between my ribs as if begging to be cut out. Other than that, he said, my lungs were like those of a man in his twenties. After all this positive news, I decided to ask him the $64,000 question. "Well, doctor, what about my John Thomas? Can he still stand up and be counted?"

"You'd better give it a go and see," he responded rather brusquely.

Undergoing a lung operation at the age of ninety was unprecedented not just in Japan, but worldwide. In a testimony to the "world record" I had set, a presentation about my operation was given at a medical conference that was held nearby. I've always liked anything dramatic, so my operation became one of my favorite stories. Plus it boosted my self-confidence. As an optimist, I always think positively about everything anyway.

✣ ✣ ✣

In the Adachi family, we tend to be long-lived. All three of my sisters are still hale and hearty. My elder sister Kame will be ninety-three this year. She's a little hard of hearing, but otherwise energetic. She's a skilled weaver and makes splash-pattern kimonos and *noren* shop curtains based on her own designs. She's good enough to teach—and she did just that until she was over eighty.

Kumano, who's a little younger than me, is the best looking of all my sisters. She was such a beauty that I used to be head over heels in love with her despite being her brother! The mere fact she had served me my bowl of rice was enough to make it taste better. Three years younger than me, she's no spring chicken now, but I still catch glimpses of her former beauty in her face.

Yasuko, my youngest sister, now lives comfortably in Nara together with her daughter-in-law and her grandchildren. After my wife died in 1970, it was Yasuko who took the greatest interest in me and looked after me. I get nostalgic at the memory of her quietly mixing paints on the seventh floor of Nichibi in Osaka! "Those were fun times," she always says of our days in the big city. Unlike me, she's clever, but emotional directness is one thing we have in common.

I'm born lucky, and I made a trouble-free recovery after the operation. I left the hospital on April 30. There were no aftereffects of any kind. In fact, I looked so well that people would ask me, "Are you sure you *really* had an operation?" I can understand why they had trouble believing it. Before the operation, even though I wasn't aware that there was anything wrong with me, obviously I couldn't have been all that healthy. People must have been able to see this. Now that the sickness had been cut out of me, it was no surprise that I looked better than ever.

"There are still plenty of things that I have to do. That's why God extended my lease on life," I would respond. I think I was able to beat the disease because I had a good balance between my body and my mind.

Ninety Years
Old and the
Dream Goes On

U ntil my lung operation this spring, I was living a life of quiet retirement. Successfully overcoming the unexpected hurdle of a major operation at age ninety encouraged and invigorated me. I feel thirty years younger. It's extraordinary how rejuvenating a newfound confidence in one's physical strength is.

I had previously composed a haiku to describe how I felt on reaching ninety. My stance was philosophical, if a little pessimistic.

> To cross the ninety-year hill,
> Is to become
> A child again.

After my operation, I felt so confident about still being in the prime of life that I revised the poem to make it more positive. Now it is about continuing to fight and drinking life's cup to the dregs.

> Though I have climbed
> The ninety-year hill,
> My dreams go on.

The late Hiragushi Denchu, a sculptor, was equally positive, famously liking to say that men in their sixties and seventies are no more than snotty-nosed boys. A man, he said, was in his prime when he turned a hundred years old! I see his point. In a society like that of contemporary Japan where most people live to an advanced age, your attitude toward life is the secret to being happy. I agree with the old saying about how it's your feelings that decide how life is going to turn out for you.

That's why I dislike it when people treat me like an old man. Okay, I admit that *physically* I'm not young, but my mind is as quick and my imagination as vivid as anybody else's.

I've been spared all the standard problems of old age—senile dementia and so on. The fact that I can still dream big dreams and feel passionate about my projects is proof of that.

The secret of good health is to keep on moving. I'm not just talking about staying physically active, but being mentally active, too. Some people find that the weaker their bodies become, the more they use their minds. Painters are an example of this. An extraordinary number of Japanese painters past the age of ninety have overcome infirmity to produce wonderful work. The old saying that compares man to a "frail, thinking reed" is spot on.

❖ ❖ ❖

One of the things I am passionate about right now is the restoration of Toda Castle on Mount Gassan in Hirose. Mount Gassan is 630 feet high. On it stood the principal castle of Amago, the warlord who was said to have toiled on behalf of the people of Izumo "with all the vigor of the rainbow" when he controlled the surrounding region during the Warring States period (1457–1568). My dream is to rebuild the castle, creating a draw for tourists and revitalizing the area.

If we stocked the rebuilt castle with medieval and modern art exhibits, I am sure that the half a million visitors who come to the Adachi Museum each year would be happy to go over there, too. To conserve the richness of nature on the site, we could plant *ume* plum trees and establish it as a place to visit on the plum-blossom trail. This is my two-pronged strategy for boosting this region's appeal.

The restored castle would also form part of the view from the Adachi Museum and thus represents a great way to get the most out of a historic ruin. Since the castle ruins were designated a place of national historic interest in 1934, my rebuilding the castle is not in the cards for now. The law for the preservation of cultural assets includes strict rules on new construction, so I am working to remove this status.

The area around the ruins of Toda Castle is also designated a prefectural natural park. At the moment, there is nothing there but a few old stone walls and some withered Japanese pampas grass blowing in the wind. It's a disappointingly shabby sight.

I was raised in Hirose so the place means a lot to me. I want to devote the rest of my life to realizing the collective dream of the people of Hirose: the restoration of Toda Castle. Because I wanted as many people as possible to see with their own eyes how the presence of a castle ennobles a landscape, I built a wooden replica of Matsue Castle on Mount Kanao.

My second dream project is the construction of a museum of contemporary art. First, I plan to dig out an artificial lake about 1,000 feet wide on the way from Saginoyu Onsen to Yasugi. Then, using the excavated earth, I intend to build an artificial island in the lake with a guesthouse for important government and cultural figures. The guesthouse will be reflected on the lake's surface like Ukimi-do temple, while Mount Daisen, the glory of our San'in region, towers up in the background.

I also plan to build a heliport nearby so that VIP guests can come and go by helicopter. I believe we are on the brink of an era when people will shuttle from city to city and town to town in high-performance helicopters. On the shore of the lake I plan to build a hotel, which I will call the Hotel Taikan, so that visitors can spend the whole day in the Adachi Museum without needing to worry about hurrying back home in the evening.

Regardless of how much you've got, money means nothing unless you use it. Money acquires meaning only when it's put to use in the real world. This is a point I always hammer home when talking to the firms I'm trying to interest in my plans. When I approach the heads of top companies to work with me in building the guesthouse and the hotel, I always explain my philosophy. "Having loads of money is no big deal. The point is, if you're going to spend that money and build something, then you want to create something that everyone will acknowledge to be unique—the best in the world. The Tokugawa shoguns built the Toshogu in Nikko as a shrine to Tokugawa Ieyasu. We should have a similar aim: to build something that will become a Japanese national treasure."

"Half-baked, wholly worthless," says the proverb, and I agree. It's better to do nothing at all than to do something commonplace. I want to revolutionize the way corporations think about culture. At the same time, I'd like the government to rethink the tax system in relation to plans like mine. Although my plans are still very much at the drawing-board stage, I am passionate about building this museum of contemporary Japanese painting to showcase living artists and turning this whole area into what I call "a giant treasure house of beauty," both natural and man-made.

From being the number one museum in the San'in region, I want us to go on to become number one in Kansai (central Japan), then number one in all Japan—until all that's left to conquer is the rest of the world. My next project is to kindle the interest of an international audience in the Adachi Museum of Art. Most foreign tourists who come to Japan these days follow a predictable course, visiting things like the Imperial Palace in Tokyo and the temples of Kyoto. I want to make sure that in the near future the next stop on their tour will be the Adachi Museum of Art. All my dreams are focused on that goal.

Present-day Japan has achieved unprecedented levels of economic growth and has earned itself an important position in the international community. Developments in Japan are important enough to have a direct and powerful influence on the global economy. While this is something that we Japanese can be proud of as a people, it's not something we can afford to become conceited about. A quick survey of how we are regarded by other countries is enough to make that clear. Their opinion of us is not as high as we might hope. I am no scholar, but I think one reason for our low standing is that Japan is not perceived as a country of culture. We focus on our position in the GNP rankings or our strength as an economic superpower, as the rest of the world looks on with distaste.

There are too few cultural facilities in Japan. Japan urgently needs to foster deeper intellectual and cultural exchanges with other nations. We must extract greater leverage from the power of our culture. Japan is blessed with one of the world's great aesthetic traditions. Even if as a nation we can't be bothered to promote it widely, the very least we can do is make sure that overseas visitors get a proper sense of Japan's splendid culture.

Naturally, I want these foreign tourists to come to the Adachi Museum of Art. I am proud of the place and believe it to be representative of Japanese culture as a whole. Nothing, in fact, would make me happier than the Adachi Museum of Art taking up its responsibility to make a positive contribution to international friendship. That is why my next goal is to increase the number of museum visitors from overseas.

I don't want to sound pretentious, but a well-balanced mind with the capacity to appreciate is a force that can overcome all obstacles. Even when countries engage in diplomatic negotiations, ultimately it's about one group of people coming face-to-face with another. And if these people have the ability to stop and smell the roses—to savor, enjoy, and appreciate things—that will influence the content and outcome of their negotiations.

Such is the power of culture. I truly believe that Japan will be on the road to a rocky future if this dream project of mine never becomes a reality. I am a passionate believer in national cultural policy.

As we're already dealing with weighty issues, I want to describe another of my recent dream projects. I have a plan to

Holding forth in the Adachi Museum of Art cafe.

construct an international conference center at Mount Nomiya, a mountain less than ten minutes from the museum by car and only about 500 feet high. I want to construct a facility that will attract scholars and figures from the world of culture not only from Japan but from all over the world.

Granted, we already have the Kyoto International Conference Center, but in an age with more and more cross-border activity, a developed country like Japan needs a more versatile, multifaceted conference center. In our new global age with its quest for world peace, there is sure to be a rise in cultural exchange and diplomatic contacts in both the government and private sector. I want to move fast to create a space to meet that need here in San'in, the best place to host such a facility.

Why am I proposing this international conference center? First off, Japan still has few such facilities of the proper quality (though recently a couple of regions began discreetly developing plans to attract investment in such a project), and second, and more important, the Izumo region has everything needed to please the overseas visitor. The area is wonderfully picturesque. There are gleaming, peaceful lakes like Nakaumi (with Daikon-shima island) and Shinji. There are the mountains of the Shimane Peninsula and the Yumigahama Peninsula, and the grand expanse of the Sea of Japan, with Okinoshima island visible in the distance. Then there is the peaceful, quiet, and luxuriantly green hilly region around Mount Nomiya.

Convenient transportation is the second factor. The two airports, Izumo Airport and Yonago Airport, are both about an hour away from the proposed site. By jet, it's only about a ninety-minute flight from Tokyo's Haneda Airport. It's also an easy journey by car with the Trans-Chugoku Highway and the Yonago-Matsue bypass.

A third point is that all the best tourist spots of San'in are close by. The National Park at Daisen, Izumo Taisha shrine, Matsue Castle, Ichibata Yakushi, Mihonoseki, and Kiyomizu-dera temple can all be reached in about an hour or less. The same is true of *onsen*, or natural hot springs, which can be found at Tamatsukuri, Matsue, Kaike, and Saginoyu. *Onsen* have a unique atmosphere that cannot be experienced outside of Japan. This makes San'in a fabulous place for resting and recharging.

Fourth, San'in is not far from Hiroshima, "the tombstone of the human race." Being close to the city that suffered the world's first nuclear bomb attack makes San'in the right place for a conference center devoted to world peace and human happiness.

Finally, the region is rich in Japanese culture. As the seat of an ancient culture, Izumo is considered to be "the root of Japan." Many bronze swords from the Yayoi period have been dug up here, and there are many unique historic sites (perhaps the best known of which is Kojindani in Hikawacho) that have attracted nationwide interest, as well as traces of Iron Age culture. I am sure an international audience would be interested in a region so rich in history.

To prepare Mount Nomiya to be an international conference center and guesthouse, we need to upgrade Yonago and Izumo into international airports, build a bridge over Lake

Nakaumi, and improve the Yonago-Matsue bypass and Trans-Chugoku Highway.

Whatever the obstacles, Japan needs to wake up to the importance of cultural policy if it wants to become a top-rank nation in fact as well as in name. Right now I am doing my best to push the surveys along so construction can start as soon as possible. My construction plans were outlined in a letter published on July 24, 1988, in the *San'in Chuo Shinpo* newspaper. I owe a great deal to Mataga Seiichi, the firm's CEO, who has given me so much wise advice regarding the museum garden and the projected conference center. Mataga has a gift for seeing through to the essence of things, and I respect him as a man of sterling character. In my efforts to make my dream a reality, I recently asked Sumita Nobuyoshi, the governor of Shimane, to set up a meeting that would bring him and the governors of Tottori and Hiroshima prefectures together to discuss the project.

The TV personality Takemura Ken'ichi, who recently came to the museum, declared himself strongly in favor of my project and offered to do what he could to help. Takemura ended up doing a segment on me called "The Dream of the Ninety-year-old Man" in his TV show *Looking at Society,* which made me even more enthusiastic about my plans.

On the subject of things I'm grateful for, I also got a lot of good advice in phone conversations with Tsunematsu Seiji, who was governor of Shimane for three terms, a total of twelve years. Since he was clever enough to be a professor at the prestigious Gakushuin University, I assumed we wouldn't get along at all; I was delighted when he called to say that he was looking forward to meeting me and picking my brains about a variety of issues. Excitable fellow that I am, I was keen to get together with him right then and there.

✢ ✢ ✢

In November 1988, the Ministry of Cultural Affairs singled me out as someone who has made significant contributions to culture in the region. I was delighted to accept this honor that recognizes the effort and achievement of individuals or organizations in promoting culture locally over many years. Plenty of people these days like to harp on about how the "age of the regions"—that is, regioncentric thinking versus centralized policy making—has come. I think that in the future the disparity between the central government and the regions will disappear. The unique characters of the different regions will boost their economic development, and they will have their own vigorous local culture.

As I have been writing about my life, one idea has stuck with me: Life is all about chance encounters. Your encounters with people and things determine how your life will play out. Since most people have strong egos, they tend to think that all their achievements are the result of their own efforts and abilities. But I believe that much of what we are comes from the people we meet in the course of our lives. In a way, it may be fairer to say that we don't really live our own lives, but are guided through them by other people.

I want to take this opportunity to say thank you to all of the many people I have met in the course of my life, and to people who are somehow linked to me even if we never met face-to-face. The bigger the project you are working on and the grander your dreams, the more aware you are of how little you could achieve by yourself.

Being properly grateful for your blessings makes you a stronger person. That may sound like the Buddhist doctrine of "dependence on other people," but there is a proactive and life-affirming attitude at its core. Being able to depend on other people is proof of an ability to assess them correctly. I want to make sure I retain these precious feelings of gratitude in the future. "Tomorrow more than today; the day after tomorrow still more than that" was the prayer Yamanaka Shikanosuke addressed to the crescent moon. Like him, I want to grow steadily wiser, and walk through my nineties humbly and without misstep.

I have always been impatient, but recently, perhaps because of my age, I've started paying more attention to other people and listening to what they have to say. I used to talk about myself without thought for the person I was talking to, but now, I always make a point of asking what I can do for them, and only then, assuming that there's time available, giving my opinion. Even at ninety, it's never too late to learn!

But I am who I am, and the leopard never really changes its spots. Habits of years don't vanish overnight. It doesn't take much for me to work up a head of steam and launch into an impassioned speech supporting my dream projects. I justify this with the argument that a person's faults are a big part of what makes each of us human, and that keeping my dreams alive in my heart will help me act as a bridge to succeeding generations.

Just above my heart, tucked into my breast pocket, sits my old school report card, a mass of Cs and Ds. Dog-eared but still mildly smug, it is always watching over me.

Conclusion

Does anyone really understand the structure and machinery of human memory? Recently, probably due to old age, mine has become rather unreliable. I can usually remember things from a few days ago, but something someone told me in the morning is likely to have vanished from my mind the same afternoon. I end up having to repeat the favorite excuse of politicians: "No, I don't remember that."

But my memory is not completely shot. There's an old Japanese folktale about a fisherman named Urashima Taro who is transported on a turtle's back to a palace at the bottom of the sea. He thinks he has only been gone a couple of days, but on returning home, he discovers that three hundred years have passed. Well, rather like him, I find that I still have a surprisingly good memory when it comes to money, women, and paintings—the things I'm *really* interested in—even for events that took place long ago. How much I paid for a piece of land or the composition, coloring, and price of every single work in my collection—this sort of information just rolls off my tongue. I'm hopeless at accounting but still good at doing sums in my head. In other words, there's been no decline at all in my ability to do the things I've always had a knack for. A chance remark or the sight of a landscape is enough to bring old memories teeming back.

I have had this experience frquently while writing this book. I say writing, but I actually dictated it into a tape-recorder—and I'm nothing if not a big talker!—and then Yoshimoto Tadanori, an art promoter, was kind enough to type up the chapters for me. I started gathering material for the book in late 1987. I dictated it in chronological order from my childhood, talking about things as they occurred to me, just as I had been advised to do. Since I'm interested in so many things, I ended up going off on all sorts of tangents and derailing the narrative, when some especially powerful memory came up. This resulted in me repeating myself and caused a lot of trouble to my assistants in this project.

I don't want anything I do to be mediocre. If I'm going to something, then I have to do it well. After all, you can't approach your own autobiography halfheartedly. Every time I was presented with the typed-up manuscript it would dredge up all sorts of forgotten memories. To be honest, I always had the niggling feeling that I wasn't quite there yet. I never really felt, "Great, that's it. That's everything. I can't do any better."

The very last thing I want to say is that I could not have achieved anything without other people's help—those people who reached out to help me when I was in trouble and those who have stuck with me loyally right up until today. I know that if I hadn't been lucky enough to meet them, I would not be where I am today and the Adachi Museum of Art would not exist. People really are the most precious asset.

Although I feel relieved to be nearly finished with my life story, I am also reluctant to say goodbye. I still feel I have more to say; on the other hand, now that I know how difficult it is to write about oneself and one's own life, I am also keen to finish as fast as I can!

This book is written from my personal point of view. It's about things as I saw or felt them. I'm a bit of a scatterbrain so there are bound to be some slips of memory and some mistakes.

But isn't that the nature of memory? People all look different from one another, so it's no surprise that we all see and remember the same things differently, according to our points of view. Nonetheless, in an effort to write something of lasting value, I have tried to be as honest and accurate about my own feelings as possible.

On December 31, 1988, as I was about to finish this book, Adachi Inosuke, my childhood friend who was three years my senior, passed away. I stood speechless with grief beside his still warm body. When his family, who was preparing the corpse, asked me to help with making him up for the funeral (he always was immaculately turned out), I could not hold back the tears.

On January 7, 1989, the Showa Emperor died. One sad bereavement follows another. I am three years older than the Showa Emperor, so I don't know how much of an effect I'll have on the new Heisei era, but I intend to take it slowly and steadily, one step at a time.

I would like to apologize to any patrons or friends of mine I failed to mention due to constraints of space or lack of narrative flow. Let me take this opportunity to thank them for their kindness.

I would also like to thank all the people who helped me produce this book.

Last but by no means least, I want to say a heartfelt "thank you" to everybody who has ever visited the Adachi Museum of Art—the customer is always king.

Now let me bring this "Chronicle of Zenko" to an end.

Afterword: Speaking for My Grandfather

by Adachi Takanori

Adachi Zenko passed away on December 19, 1990, at the age of ninety-two. He continued to pursue his dreams up to the end, doing his utmost to establish a new contemporary art museum and an international conference center near the Adachi Museum of Art. He never lost his enthusiasm for meeting new people and for great works of art. There was something humbling for the rest of us in his inexhaustible vitality. I recall the epic highs and lows of his life and his passionate dedication to his dreams with sadness tinged with envy.

Reading this autobiography awoke many memories of my grandfather. These memories make me all the more conscious of the responsibility I bear as one of the team now responsible for managing his museum. This renewed exposure to my grandfather's larger-than-life personality also makes me aware of my own inadequacies. For me, this book is less a memento of my late grandfather than an indispensable reference book for the job I have to do.

My grandfather's whole life can be distilled to the one essential act of establishing the Adachi Museum of Art. He was a man whose life was a series of full-frontal assaults, but in later years, especially after his decision to build a museum here in Furukawa, Yasugi, he gradually mellowed. He became more tolerant, more understanding, more sensitive, and better at getting on with people.

Daily contact with magnificent works of art smoothed the rougher edges of his character, and he developed a deeper sense of what he owed to others. He became more conscious of the value of the people he met and the friendships he was able to enjoy with them. He was especially anxious to give something back to the society that had given him so much, and did his best to help create jobs and support social welfare for the local population. He developed an acute sense of the power that culture has to unite people. "When people tell me how much they like the museum, it just makes me more determined to develop it into a top-level, world-class museum that will give even more pleasure to more people," my grandfather often used to say.

Of course, he was deeply committed to the museum he had founded, but I see the museum as an expression of the drive of a man who loved beauty deeply. He adored Yokoyama Taikan, but it was sheer grit and determination that enabled him to build up so important a collection that this museum is often referred to as the "Yokoyama Taikan Museum."

The museum had already acquired *Mount Fuji* and *Summer* from Taikan's highly regarded *Ten Scenes of the Sea and Ten Scenes of Mount Fuji* series, but in spring 2003, more than a decade after the death of my grandfather, two more works from this series came to light, *Dragon and Mount Fuji* and *Autumn*. The two pictures were known as the "phantom masterpieces" because their whereabouts were unknown for sixty years. There were plenty of complications along the way, but eventually we acquired them and brought them back to the museum, rather like a groom bringing his bride back to his house. Our purchase of these two works involved some almost miraculous twists of fate.

Almost immediately after the news of the discovery of *Dragon and Mount Fuji* broke in the newspapers, the picture was sent off to auction. The Adachi Museum prides itself on being one of the leading museums of Taikan's work, so we desperately wanted to make a successful bid. The trouble was, we knew we did not have the financial resources to compete. It was frustrating and humiliating.

But when we had abandoned hope, someone approached us proposing that we should buy not only *Dragon and Mount Fuji* but *Autumn* as well, thus acquiring both the lost works in one go. I simply could not believe my ears. The dealer explained that the collector who owned both works liked the mission of the Adachi Museum so much that he had decided it was the best place for his Taikans to go. I was so thrilled I got goose bumps!

During his lifetime, my grandfather often said, "If any work from the *Ten Scenes of the Sea and Ten Scenes of Mount Fuji* series comes onto the market, forget about everything else and buy it." I was delighted to be able to add these two "phantom masterpieces" to the Adachi Collection. I also felt that my grandfather's single-minded enthusiasm (he always said that Taikan was his "lifelong love") made things turn out as wonderfully as they did. Other institutions were able to offer far more than we could, but the prestige of the Adachi Museum and its strong link with the work of Yokoyama Taikan were enough to swing things in our favor. The upshot was that we now had a total of eight works from *Ten Scenes of the Sea and Ten Scenes of Mount Fuji*, and our Yokoyama Taikan collection became even more significant.

To commemorate the discovery of these two masterpieces, an exhibition entitled *Yokoyama Taikan: Ten Subjects on Seas and Mountains, Respectively* was held first at the University Art Museum of Tokyo University of the Arts (July 27–August 29, 2004) and then at the Adachi Museum of Art (September 3–September 26, 2004).

This exhibition was of historic importance in that it united all twenty works from the series in one place—something that may never happen again. I am sure my grandfather, wherever he is now, wept with joy at the sight.

Voted Japan's Number 1 Garden

We got another nice surprise not long after our acquisition of these two works. *The Journal of Japanese Gardening (JOJG)* is a bimonthly American magazine distributed in thirty-seven countries worldwide, with English-speaking countries as its main market. In the magazine's first-ever ranking of Japanese gardens, the Adachi Museum of Art had been designated number one. (Incidentally, Katsura Imperial Villa in Kyoto took second place.)

The panel consisted of gardening experts from Japan, the U.S., and Australia who had visited gardens in some fifty locations in Japan over the previous ten-year period. They made a comprehensive assessment of 389 gardens around Japan from every possible angle: the quality of the garden, how it harmonized with the buildings in it, the treatment of visitors, garden maintenance and management, and the courtesy of the individual staffers.

When compiling its rankings, the *JOJG* refuses to be bound by the conventional wisdom that a "proper" Japanese garden has to be in Kyoto, or has to have historical associations. As such, it was the first-ever attempt to evaluate Japanese gardens more objectively. The results also meant more because the panel of judges was not composed exclusively of Japanese people. Many of the judges were lavish in their praise of the Adachi Museum's garden, calling it a "tour de force of meticulous maintenance."

I cannot even begin to imagine how happy this would have made my grandfather. I myself was delighted, while also being a little awestruck at the sheer force of my grandfather's will, which continued to pursue—and realize—his grand dreams and ambitions even beyond the grave.

The newspapers in Japan all had a field day reporting that the garden of the Adachi Museum of Art had taken the number one spot at the expense of celebrated Kyoto landmarks like Nijo Castle, Shisen-do, Kinkakuji, and, of course, Katsura Imperial Villa,. There was a surge in the number of people accessing our Web site, and magazines started running more features about the museum. There was enormous interest in the sort of man my grandfather had been, and how he had created such a splendid museum and garden.

My grandfather was not an art-school graduate, nor did he have any training in gardening. In a sense, he was nothing more than an amateur. That such a man created a museum and garden of so high a quality is nothing short of a miracle. He was intensely passionate in the pursuit of anything he had set his sights on, but he also had extraordinary levels of intuition and insight. He was an amateur on a heroic scale who understood the essence of beauty—and that was why he was able to achieve what he did.

The *JOJG* ranks Japanese gardens on an annual basis, and has ranked the Adachi Museum number one seven years running since it started to publish its rankings. The scale of the survey keeps growing: the first survey examined 389 gardens, the third, 632, and the seventh, 827.

On October 1, 2008 the first new edition in thirteen years of *Guide Bleu Japon* (a French guidebook to Japan) was published, and it awarded the Adachi Museum of Art three stars, its highest ranking. The *Guide Bleu*, comparable to the Michelin guides, grades places with three ("must see"), two ("very interesting"), one ("interesting"), or zero stars. The profile of the Adachi Museum included a photograph and proved that our being "the best garden in Japan" is no idle boast.

The *Guide Vert*, the guide of French rival Michelin, also awarded the Adachi Museum's garden three stars, the highest rating, while giving the museum itself two stars. The *Guide Vert* series contains 325 titles published in nine languages with around 1.5 million copies in print. We initially got word that the museum had been awarded two stars but were later thoroughly delighted to hear that the garden had independently won three stars itself. As we were just about to be selected as the finest garden in Japan for the seventh consecutive year by the *JOJG*, I honestly felt that nothing less than three stars would do—Michelin's grading of us was a great relief.

In February 2009, the Japan Tourism Agency appointed me a "Yokoso Japan ambassador," making me responsible for helping them with their campaign to boost the number of overseas tourists. People who "have contributed to publicizing Japan's attractions and given a warm reception to tourists from overseas" are selected for this role. The Adachi Museum has been offering discounted admission to foreign visitors since 1992, and in 2006 was the first Japan museum to be designated as a "Visit Japan Information Center" for foreign tourists. The agency obviously liked the environment we had created for tourists and the way our Japanese garden was helping to propagate Japanese culture.

A Relaxing Museum for Everyone to Enjoy

My grandfather believed that a Japanese garden should be like a beautiful painting. He poured his heart and soul into the creation of a palace of Japanese art that combined Japanese paintings with a Japanese garden. The garden's selection as Japan's finest marked the fulfillment of a long-cherished dream.

The garden of the Adachi Museum of Art currently consists of the Reception Garden, which is the first thing that visitors see; the elegant and artistic Moss Garden; the Dry

Landscape Garden, which fuses artificial and natural beauty; the Pond Garden with its hillocks and pond; the White Gravel and Pine Garden inspired by the works of Yokoyama Taikan; and the garden of the Juryu-an Teahouse, which is modeled on the Shokin-tei Teahouse of Katsura Imperial Villa.

Probably no other museum anywhere can boast such a number and variety of Japanese gardens within a single site. My grandfather lavished care on these gardens morning, noon, and night, and they are the physical expression of his passion and sense of purpose. His zeal infuses every tree, every shrub, and every piece of gravel in the garden. Not just the gardeners but all the museum staff, who perform tasks like picking up dead leaves and raking the gravel, preserve this precious passion.

The Adachi Museum of Art is open year-round, and we receive visitors every day of the year. We need to be doubly careful about maintaining and grooming the garden to ensure that visitors can come and view it anytime without risk of disappointment. The aim is to create a landscape that follows seamlessly from the museum's Japanese paintings, without spoiling the mood or introducing any discordant notes. Our basic concept was to create an oasis of the heart, a place where all people can relish an idealized native landscape and savor art and nature equally. There's no theorizing or rationalizing about art here. The moment you step into the museum building you are freed from the hassle of everyday things; you are in a space of total tranquillity and peace of mind. That is the Adachi Museum of Art.

On January 9, 2004, we erected a plaque to commemorate our being voted the number one garden in Japan. It stands in a corner of the garden beside the statue of my grandfather, which points to the Pond Garden, the Dry Landscape Garden, and the gentle curving outlines of the mountains beyond. I am sure that my grandfather is enjoying the way the garden looks different every minute of the day, smiling benignly down from the other world with that smile of which he was so proud.

I was thrilled at the Adachi Museum being selected as Japan's best garden for seven years in succession, a distinction that led to a dramatic rise on our profile, and a clear increase in our overseas visitor numbers. At the same time, mingled with my delight is a heavy sense of responsibility. We now need to take even greater care in our efforts to create and maintain a beautiful Japanese garden so that it can continue to be worthy of this honor.

The Adachi Museum of Art Award

The Adachi Museum's business plan is based on the wishes of my late grandfather. It includes a plan for a new gallery of contemporary *nihonga* (traditional Japanese painting) focusing on artists from the Showa period (1926–89). We intend to open this new gallery in the basement and the second floor of the current building on November 3, 2010, to mark the museum's fortieth anniversary. On display will be major works by around eighty important contemporary artists, with a focus on Hirayama Ikuo of the Japan Art Institute; Miyasako Masaaki, who was born locally; and paintings that have received the Adachi Museum of Art Award, given to works featured in our spring and autumn exhibitions. The concept is to provide a systematic overview of the evolution of contemporary *nihonga*. I hope that this will add a whole new dimension to the identity of the museum.

To generate excitement, we plan to hold two exhibitions simultaneously: the 95th Reorganized Inten Exhibition, the annual exhibition of the Japan Art Institute (for two weeks beginning on November 3, 2010); and a Yokoyama Taikan exhibition (using all the exhibition space in the current museum). Yokoyama Taikan participated in the formation of the Japan

Art Institute, and I am sure the public will enjoy seeing how contemporary artists have reinterpreted his legacy and will appreciate the vigorous dialogue between old and new.

The Adachi Museum of Art Award was founded together with the Japan Art Institute in 1995 and is awarded at the Inten Exhibition, held in the autumn of every year. The award-winning work is purchased by the museum and added to the collection. The following are the winners to date each year: Nishida Shun'ei, Maehara Mitsuo, Kishino Kaori, Ide Yasuto, Odano Naoyuki, Yoshimura Seiji, Hokari Haruo, Miyakita Chiori, Kurashima Shigetomo, Muraoka Kimio, Kadoshima Naoki, Nishida Shun'ei (again), Yamada Shin, and Nakamura Yuzuru. Of these, five painters—Nishida Shun'ei, Yoshimura Seiji, Kadoshima Naoki, Odano Naoyuki, and Miyakita Chiori—have been elected to the executive committee of the Japan Art Institute. In 2005, the Adachi Museum of Art Award was introduced for the spring Inten Exhibition. Yoshimura Seiji won the first award. Later winners include Murakami Yuji, Matsumura Koji, Mori Midori, and Muraoka Kimio.

I am on the selection committee for the awards. The uniformly high standard of the winning works always gives me a renewed awareness of the quality of the artists who participate in the Inten Exhibition. I hope that everyone who sees the pictures feels the novelty and freshness of contemporary art.

My youngest daughter, Adachi Tomomi, had her first painting, a work called *Appearances*, accepted for the Inten Exhibition of spring 2005; a second, called *Memory of a Dream*, for the spring Inten Exhibition in 2007; and a third, *Lullaby on a Moonlit Night*, in the 2009 spring Inten exhibition. In the autumn 2009 Inten Exhibition her *The Origin of Life* was selected for the first time. I hope that a combination of the study of her predecessors and the contemplation of nature will help her go far.

Faithful to My Grandfather's Wishes

The Adachi Museum of Art's basic philosophy is to cultivate the seeds that my grandfather originally sowed, help them flower, and get as many people as possible to enjoy them and see what the museum stands for. Eighteen years have passed since my grandfather died. The time has gone by amazingly fast. Nonetheless, my grandfather's spirit lives on inside of me and grows ever stronger. As both director of the museum and the head of the museum trustees, I am always trying to figure out what steps we need to take to become the world-class museum my grandfather wanted us to be.

Recently I have started to think of the museum as a living thing. That may sound a little abstract, but I have begun to grasp that just as the Japanese garden looks different at different times of the day, so the artworks in our museum also produce a different impression, depending on the emotional state or living environment of the viewer. The truly splendid things on this earth—whether a garden or a work of art—possess a life force that transcends time and space.

The Adachi Museum of Art is committed to carrying out with the wishes of its founder. My mission is thus to communicate the splendor of my grandfather's double legacy of modern *nihonga* and Japanese gardens to the wider world. In an age where social fragmentation and digitization are advancing by leaps and bounds, there is meaning and value to be found in handmade beauty and in the physical preservation of works of art. It may be a painstaking business, but it speaks to something deep inside us all.

I wanted to take advantage of the publication of this book to give a brief overview of what is going on at the museum, and to articulate the gratitude I feel toward my grandfather for all his kindness and support. I hope this Afterword has added another dimension to your image of Adachi Zenko as a man and given you an understanding of the museum's philosophy. The entire staff of the museum is devoted to making the museum even better to ensure that you, the reader, will visit us not just once but repeatedly.

Last of all, I would like to take this opportunity to thank Suko Shinji, formerly of Nihon Keizai Shimbun-sha, Genseki Takashi of Nihon Keizai Shimbun-sha, and Shiraishi Masaru and Yoshino Asako of Nihon Keizai Shimbun Shuppan-sha, who all played a major role in arranging for the publication of this book.

I look forward to welcoming you to the Adachi Museum of Art.

November 2009
Adachi Takanori
Director of the Adachi Museum of Art
and Chairman of the Board of Trustees

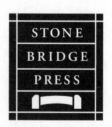

This and other fine titles published by Stone Bridge Press are available from booksellers worldwide and online.
sbp@stonebridge.com • www.stonebridge.com